KU-216-133

Catching the Light

These teaching materials have been produced with the generous support of Reed International.

REED INTERNATIONAL

© WWF UK 1991

All rights reserved. No part of this publication may be reproduced, stored in a retrieval system, or transmitted in any form or by any means electronic, mechanical, photocopying, recording or otherwise, without the prior permission of WWF UK.

WWF UK
Panda House
Weyside Park
Godalming, Surrey
GU7 1XR

ISBN: 0 947613 30 7

Designed by: Schermuly Design Co., London
Typeset and printed by: Manor Park Press Ltd.
Cover Illustration: Jane Ray
Photography — Rainforest frieze and hedgehog homes and display: Alan Jones

Catching the Light

BRIAN MOSES

Contents

INTRODUCTION 6

THE CHILD 10

THE NEIGHBOURHOOD 20

THE SCHOOL 30

TOWNS AND CITIES 38

THE COUNTRYSIDE 46

PARKS AND PLAYGROUNDS 56

THE SEASHORE 62

WATER 70

WASTE AND RECYLING 82

ENDANGERED ANIMALS 90

FURTHER READING 102

FURTHER READING RESOURCES FOR TEACHERS AND PUPILS 102

USEFUL ADDRESSES FOR RESOURCE MATERIAL 104

SELECTED EDUCATIONAL VISITS 105

ACKNOWLEDGEMENTS 108

Catching the Light

Catching the light
Catching the light
Shining bright
Day and night
Catching the light.

Shine its beam into the dark
Light up the truth for each other
Fan the flame, kindle the spark
I'm your sister, I'm your brother
Let's catch the light.

Take my meat, my fish, my bread
We share one skin, we share one blood
My eyes, your face, my heart, your head
End the hunger, share the food
Let's catch the light.

Let the light fill up the skies
To flood the Earth, the trees and streams
No more waste, or war, or lies
Catch the light and share my dreams
Let's catch the light.

Spin the light into a ball
Of hope and laughter, dance and rhyme
We'll throw it round between us all
Share our world, our space, our time
Let's catch the light.

Catching the light
Catching the light
Shining bright
Day and night
Let's catch the light.

DAVID HARMER

Introduction

A DECENT FUTURE for all of us now can only come about through the rediscovery of our environment. We need to learn to value differences as well as similarities and to develop the kind of global awareness that helps us to understand how the world itself is greater than the sum of its many parts. We should perhaps reflect on some words of Chief Standing Bear: 'The Old Lakota was wise. He knew that man's heart away from nature becomes hard; he knew that lack of respect for growing, living things soon led to lack of respect for humans too.' (Lakota—tribal name for the western bands of Plains people now known as the Sioux.)

During the last decade it has become increasingly obvious that children are exhibiting great concern about what is happening in the world. Television programmes such as *Blue Peter* and *Newsround* have alerted children in Britain to the suffering of children in other countries. *Blue Peter* appeals have generated wave after wave of compassion that has translated itself into local action on unprecedented scales. Quite often too, it is children who have concerned themselves with such issues as the depletion of the ozone layer and the destruction of rainforests, encouraging their parents to switch to environmentally friendly products that in some small way might help to lessen the damage.

If the media is helping to shape children's awareness of environmental issues and to suggest avenues for action, then schools must surely have a vital role to play in the production of long term programmes of learning which are geared to inform and to encourage the expression of opinion. Increasingly research indicates that such a programme requires implementation and development from the moment that children enter school as reception infants.

Environmental awareness is cross-curricular and every subject has some part to play in equipping children with the knowledge and skills that are needed for them to be able to formulate and justify their own views on human activity and its effects on the world we live in. It is particularly desirable for work on the environment to be integrated into core curriculum areas such as language where talking, listening, reading and writing activities can assist children in consideration and clarification of their feelings towards important issues.

Discussion can initially be focused on the extent of local problems—how much vandalism takes place in a nearby park, what can be done about litter in the town centre? Such speculative discussion can lead to action. Publicity campaigns can be mounted to make others aware of wider issues—the vanishing rhino, rainforest destruction or the need for clean water in Nepal or Nigeria.

Much talking and listening should, of course, take place at all stages, with children learning to appreciate that it is just as important to listen to someone else's viewpoint as it is to put across their own. Discussion groups should vary in size and composition, with a range of tasks being set that allow children to consider different ways of managing the environment. Through the debate and exploration of issues, children will begin to understand not only that different points of view exist but also that a final answer cannot always be guaranteed.

Throughout *Catching the Light* there are suggestions as to picture books and other stories that are suited to the age range. These in themselves are rich and stimulating reads, and many of them are directly concerned with an environmental issue of some kind. Indications are then given as to the kind of talking and writing that could well result from the sharing of such texts, and hopefully assist in the development of responsible attitudes towards the environment. There are also suggested activities to encourage close observation of the natural world where discussion and written work can heighten the common experience.

Catching the Light also includes reports of work by teachers who are tackling environmental issues with young children through drama, role play and imaginative writing. There are original pieces of prose and poetry from both adult writers and children which may, in turn, act as stimuli to writing in the classroom. There are suggestions as to project activities that could foster environmental awareness whilst at the same time fulfilling many of the National Curriculum's attainment targets for English at Key stages 1 and 2.

It is hoped that through these and similar activities, awareness and curiosity about the environment may be aroused and active involvement in environmental issues encouraged.

BRIAN MOSES.

Attainment targets which children may be helped to achieve through work suggested in 'Catching The Light'.

ATI — SPEAKING & LISTENING

	a	b	c	d	e	f
Level 1	●	●	●			
2	●	●	●	●	●	
3	●	●	●	●		
4	●	●	●	●		

AT2 — READING

	a	b	c	d	e	f
Level 1	●	●	●	●		
2				●	●	●
3	●	●	●	●	●	●
4	●	●	●	●		

AT3 — WRITING

	a	b	c	d	e	f
Level 1	●					
2	●	●	●	●		
3	●	●	●	●	●	
4	●	●	●	●	●	

The Child

Me

According to
My family
I have:

Dad's nose
Mum's eyes
Uncle Bob's mouth
Auntie Jean's chin
Grandpa's legs
Granny's hair
Sister Lucy's hands
Brother Paul's feet
and Cousin Rita's knees

But no one
Can explain where
I get this
Peculiar feeling

This feeling
Of being

Me

TONY BRADMAN

WHEN CHILDREN first attend school, the skilful infant teacher will be promoting self-esteem and building confidence in a variety of ways. In her book *Learning Together: Global Education 4 - 7* (Stanley Thornes/WWF 1990), Susan Fountain writes: *'A healthy sense of self-esteem forms the cornerstone for constructive relationships with others. Children who view themselves in a positive light are more likely to see others positively as well.'*

Obviously children will not be 'good' at everything they attempt in school and it is important to build confidence from the things that they can do well. In the first week or so, with a new class, particularly with a reception class where everyone is getting to know everyone else, examine differences and similarities. Ask two children to stand up, or stand on chairs, while the rest of the class ask them questions or point out obvious ways in which the two children are alike and ways in which they are different — Sarah has a younger brother but Karen doesn't, Karen is older than Sarah, Karen's birthday is in October and Sarah's is in November, Sarah is taller than Karen etc.

Stress how similar everyone is but also how different. Examine the particular talents that children have — Sarah rides her pony, Karen is learning ballet. Ask children to think of one particular skill that they have acquired and one that they would like to acquire. Talk about the reasons why some children can do one thing while others can't. Continue to boost self-confidence by emphasising our uniqueness as individuals.

Perhaps children from other cultures and ethnic groups could bring items of interest, which reflect their distinctiveness to school. These could then be presented in a positive light to other members of the class. Items might include a special piece of clothing, a type of food, or something associated with a particular festival.

In the following piece, Crystal Stainton writes about a skill that she has acquired:

Tip-toe

With my feet I can tip-toe

Tip-toe

I tip-toe in the night
I tip-toe in the playground

With my feet I can tip-toe

Tiptoe

CRYSTAL STAINTON (AGE 8)

Older children might try to list their own good and bad qualities, perhaps by setting them out in two columns:

Good qualities	Bad qualities
Often friendly	Can be moody
Helpful (sometimes)	Bit of a temper
Can be caring	Fights with brother
Polite	Could be tidier

Suggest that children prepare data sheets about themselves, what they can and can't do, what they would like to learn to do in the coming school year. At its simplest, a data sheet might look something like this:

My name is..

I live at ....

My age is ....

I'm good at ....

I'd like to be better at ....

I wish I didn't ....

I get angry when ....

This could be extended to include — somewhere I'd like to go, something that makes me laugh, something I wouldn't want to do, something I couldn't do before I came to school etc. The latter idea helps to promote an understanding that learning is developmental.

Much talking and listening should take place at all stages with children learning that it is just as important to listen to someone else's piece of news as it is to tell everyone theirs. Encourage children to talk about things they remember prior to coming to school. Suggest that baby brothers or sisters might visit (with their mums or dads) and that everyone could watch them being bathed or fed in the classroom. This could lead to many *I remember when . . .* stories and again, an appreciation that new skills develop as we grow up: 'I couldn't do this when I was that age!' Similar interaction could be achieved in a forward looking direction by linking up infant children with those in the lower junior years, 'When I'm that age, I'll be able to do that . . .'.

The theme of same, but different could result in some talking and writing in pairs:

I'm different from my friend:

I like .... but she likes ....

I dislike .... but she dislikes ....

I eat .... but she eats ....

I go .... but she goes ....

I play .... but she plays ....
etc

I'm the same as my friend:

We both like ....

We both dislike ....
etc.

Discuss the notion of 'being yourself'. Are there times when we can really 'be ourselves' and not have to worry about what others think of us or how our behaviour will affect others? Parents often say, 'She's so different at home, I can't believe she's so good at school.' Discuss with the children whether they wear different faces at home to the ones they wear at school. Writing might take the form of:

At home I'm ....

but at school I'm ....

Consider how we all wear different hats and behave in different ways according to the situation in which we find ourselves. Ask children to bring photographs to school and to mount these in the centre of a piece of paper. Around the photograph can be written the various relationships that the children have with other family members and the particular interests they have that lead them to behave in different ways:

KAREN

MEMBER OF LITTLE RIDGE SCHOOL

SARAH'S COUSIN

MEMBER OF HERRING GULLS' CLASS

AUNTIE JANE'S NIECE

JENNY'S FRIEND

GRANDAD'S GRANDDAUGHTER

GRANDMA'S GRANDDAUGHTER

MEMBER OF RYE DANCE GROUP

MOTHER'S DAUGHTER

FATHER'S DAUGHTER

Alternatively, children might illustrate how they present themselves to others when they follow various interests:

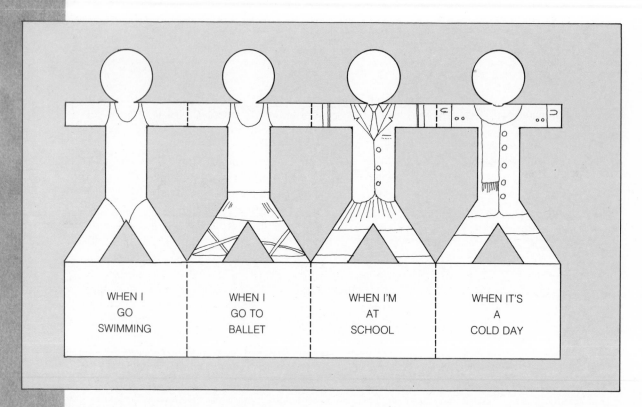

| WHEN I GO SWIMMING | WHEN I GO TO BALLET | WHEN I'M AT SCHOOL | WHEN IT'S A COLD DAY |

Encourage some children to write simple poems about themselves. Discuss what might be included and keep the lines short:

Me

I'm a girl.
I'm four foot six.
I'm eight.
I'm thin.
I'm out of this world.
I'm mad.
I'm lucky.
I'm a maths lover.
I'm somebody else.
I'm not just boring old Jessie.
I'm me.
I'm here.
I want to be me.

JESSIE ECCLES (AGE 8)

Other children might prefer to elaborate a little more on their likes and dislikes. Encourage the inclusion of small details that really give the reader an insight into the writer. Read the following piece by Flora Carnwath and point out how she extends her ideas. Instead of simply writing *'I love playing hide and seek'* she develops this so that we can feel that we are joining in too: *'I love playing hide and seek in the bracken and hearing the crackling sound all around me and jumping on rocks, gleaming among bilberry plants and wet moss . . .'.* And then also in the last two lines where she tells us why she likes cold winter evenings: *'. . . I feel cosy inside my house, toasting my toes in front of a blazing fire and eating crumpets.'*

Me

My name is Flora Carnwath, but I am called all sorts of other names like Dora or Sausage and once my cousin said, "Would you like to be called Flossie?" and then I was furious, and I sometimes feel I would like to be called Isobel which reminds me of a bowl of peaches, mangoes and pears and other luscious fruit like that. I really do not know why because Isobel is a common, everyday name. I like spaghetti because it is long and snakelike and twists in different ways. Sometimes when my mother has given me something I really want which somebody wants to swap with me I do not swap it, and often I am so bored that nothing can interest me at all, so I just loll about and draw pictures I do not want to do. Often I feel neglected and I run up to my bedroom and think about the sea with dots of white foam on small, lapping waves and sandy beaches with little flowers of rainbows hues. I love playing hide and seek in the bracken and hearing the crackling sound all around me and jumping on rocks, gleaming among bilberry plants and wet moss, and I love looking out on a summer's day and seeing white, fluffy clouds which I feel I could bounce on. I hate doing my violin practice but I love playing in an orchestra and I hate going for walks on cold, dreary winter days when I am feeling floppy. I like staying up late which I regret in the mornings because I feel stiff and tired and I like cold winter evenings when I feel cosy inside my house, toasting my toes in front of a blazing fire and eating crumpets.

YOUNG WORDS 1985 (MACMILLAN)

In Rachel Warner's *Our Class* (Hamish Hamilton 1987) children from Class 4C of Park Walk Primary School in Chelsea talk about their families, their likes and dislikes, their ambitions and their relationships with other members of the class. Something similar could be produced as a class project incorporating drawings and photographs along with the children's own comments about things that are important to them.

Older children might move on from writing about themselves to writing about another member of class, perhaps somebody they don't normally work with. Talk with the children about what kind of information might be interesting and collectively devise an interview sheet. In the following piece, Hayley asks Milton about his best time, his ambition, his likes, fears, pets, family, age, favourite toy, animal, colour and so on. She then records his answers.

Who's who in Class 7

Milton
Milton's best time was going rafting.
Milton's ambition is to be a doctor.
Milton likes fishing and dislikes small fish.
His fears are spelling tests and crocodiles.
Milton was born in Pembury hospital.
He has got one brother and two sisters.
His pets are two fish, one duck and four guinea pigs.
Milton is ten years old.
Milton loves himself, and frogs, toads, snails, caterpillars and worms, and his mum and dad.
Milton's house is not for sale.

Milton's favourite animal is a dragon fish.
His favourite colours are red, green and blue.
Milton has made a secret invention.
His favourite toy is Lego.
His collection is fishing rods.
Milton is going to Beacon school after this school.

HAYLEY BURTON (AGE 9)

Co-operation at a younger level is promoted at every stage of the day — learning to take turns with a popular activity, learning to be first in line one day, but last in line the next day, learning to share crayons, paints etc. Where someone acts in an anti-social manner, then this can be commented on by other children who will need to be led towards the making of positive and helpful comments rather than a simple condemnation.

Activities such as *Who's who in class,* where children work in different groupings, are designed to foster co-operation in the classroom. This is also the case when groups of children record the results of an activity together. Again, in her book, *Learning Together,* Susan Fountain writes of co-operative learning having '*far-reaching implications for relationships within the class.*' In group situations, children forget any notions of keeping to friends of the same gender or ethnic groupings as everyone pools their individual talents for the good of the group. This, of course, can only lead towards '*a later understanding of the interdependent nature of relationships between ethnic groups and countries . . .*'.

Family

There is only one man in the world
and his name is All Men.
There is only one woman in the world
and her name is All Women.
There is only one child in the world
and the child's name is All Children

CARL SANDBURG

Ask the children to bring to school pictures or photographs of children in other lands. Talk about the pictures. How are the children similar to us and how do they differ? Has anyone ever visited another country and played with children there? What sort of games did you play? Draw on any first-hand experiences and let those children talk to the class or answer their questions.

Read the children plenty of accounts of children in other countries. *Looking at Other Children* by Jean and David Gadsby (A. & C. Black 1980) examines the lives of several children including Ipauka of the Amazon Forest, Enok of Greenland, Mei of China and Ibrahim of Nigeria. Comparisons can be made immediately when the children hear that Ashok of India eats rice at nearly every meal, flavoured with spices or pickles. How do they feel about Ashok missing out on such delights as fishfingers and alphabet chips? There are nine people in Ashok's family who share a small house along with their animals. How does this compare with the way that we live?

Record the information in sentences:

Ashok eats rice and fish for lunch, I eat meat and potatoes.
There are nine members of Ashok's family, there are four people in my family.

Alternatively, record the information as a series of pictures with captions.

In groups, ask the children to draw up a list of the things that children need, wherever they are, so that they can grow up safe from worry and fear. A home, to be looked after, good food to eat, somewhere to sleep, to feel happy, to feel wanted, a good school, friends, being fussed over when you're ill, plenty of toys to play with and things to do — these were some of the answers that I was given by six and seven year olds.

More specific needs are listed by a secondary school student from Tanzania concerning requirements for children in his country:

Balanced diet, more schools with plenty of books and desks, clean water, medicine, clothes, toys, sweets, chocolate, biscuits, shoes and socks, sweaters, cars for their parents, video and TV sets.

Read the above list to the class. How many of these are taken for granted by children in Britain?

Most children, even the very youngest, will already have formed some notion that there are parts of the world where children lead very different lives to British children. Recently there has been much publicity concerning the plight of orphans in Romania and most children will have gained some insight into the dreadful conditions through watching programmes such as *Newsround*. Other children may be aware of the problems faced by children in many African and Asian countries. Perhaps some children have experiences to relate about helping to raise money for *Blue Peter* appeals.

How do charities try to help in countries where the needs of children are not being met? Can the children think of any charities which are particularly concerned with helping children — UNICEF, Save the Children, The Children's Society etc. Some children might like to write to a children's charity asking about their work. Alternatively, a class letter could be composed. Perhaps someone who works for a charity could visit and talk about ways in which money is collected, and how it is spent.

Reading Resources

Poetry

Heard it in the Playground by Allan Ahlberg, particularly *Things I have been doing lately*. Children may enjoy writing in a similar way (Viking 1989).

I Like That Stuff: Poems from many cultures, selected by Morag Styles. First section *Me, Myself and Others* particularly useful (CUP 1984).

The Mad Family selected by Tony Bradman (Blackie 1987).

You Just Can't Win: Poems of Family Life selected by Brian Moses (to be published by Blackie, Sept. 1991).

Fiction

Once There Were Giants by Martin Waddell and Penny Dale (Walker Books 1989). A lovely story about growing up and becoming one of the giants!

My Mum and Our Dad by Rose Impey and Maureen Galvani (Viking 1990). What children like about their mums and dads and vice versa. Plenty of stimulus to encourage the sharing of family anecdotes.

Sometimes I Wish by John Moore and Martin Wright (Deutsh 1989). 'Sometimes I Wish that when a big boy bullies me I could . . . change into a MONSTER and chase him away for ever.' Lots of techniques for dealing with different situations. Again, good stimulus material.

This Is Me by Corinne and John Rowley. (Julia MacRae 1990). A young girl thinking about what she is, and what she'd like to be. Could be good stimulus material in the classroom.

Non-fiction

Delhi Visit by Ann Morris and *Uzma's Photo Album* by Heidi Larson (A. & C. Black 1989). Two books which encourage children to share different cultural experiences.

Looking at Other Children by Jean and David Gadsby (A. & C. Black 1980). A look at the lives of children in different countries including Ipauka of the Amazon Forest and Ibrahim of Nigeria.

For Teacher: *Learning Together: Global Education 4 - 7* by Susan Fountain (Stanley Thornes/WWF 1990). Already mentioned in text but worth mentioning again as it is packed with practical ideas for fostering self-esteem, developing communication skills and promoting co-operation.

The Neighbourhood

TALK ABOUT the types of homes that we live in — houses, flats, bungalows, cottages etc. Explain what is meant by detached, semi-detached and terraced houses. Make up a chart to see who lives where. Are there children who live in homes that don't fit into this classification? Mark where children live on a large street map. Ask the children to bring to school pictures, photographs and models of houses and make up a display. Talk about unusual homes — oast houses, Martello Towers, disused railway stations. Have the children ever stayed anywhere that was a little different or do they know of anywhere?

What do the children know about houses around the world? In many countries houses are built with bricks, stone or concrete blocks — what materials are often used to build houses in many African countries or in India? What are igloos made from ? How do people choose the sort of building material that they need for their houses?

In pairs, children could compare two pictures of houses, making a list of similarities and differences. Which of the houses would they prefer to live in and why? If children could change one thing about the houses they live in, what would it be? Would it be the location, the number of rooms, the age or something else? Where would they want to live if they had a choice? Some children might enjoy writing about an ideal house.

What sort of questions might be asked if we wanted to know something about someone's house? Make up a class list. In pairs (perhaps children who don't usually work together) pupils could ask questions to discover as much as they can about their partner's home, writing down their answers or drawing pictures with captions to put across the information.

Are there any houses nearby that are being built? If so, then plan a visit. Arrange this through the site foreman and stress safety aspects — children may have to wear hard hats. Prior to the visit discover what the children already know about house building. Try to list the different stages in building a house and put them into some sort of order. This can be done as a group activity and lists can then be compared. A final list can then be agreed by the whole class. If possible, show the children's list to the site foreman or one of his colleagues and ask for comments. Have the children forgotten anything? List too, the various workmen who are engaged in house building, from the architect through to the decorator.

Ask the children to think about what else you will be aiming to find out from the visit and how this could be achieved. Perhaps photographs can be taken to show the different stages in house building. A tape recorder might be useful to record various impressions on the spot. Samples of the various materials used in house building would be useful additions to a display of work. These can then be labelled and exhibited in the sequence in which they are used. Ask the children to spend five minutes or so noting down all the various sounds that they hear on the site. These can then be incorporated into the children's writing:

Slurping, crashing goes the JCB struggling through the mud, grinding, scrunching, clashing and rubbing against other pieces of machinery. Voices bellow, hands signalling, hammers banging and the grinding of the cement mixer. Men deafened by the humming of machinery, screeching of brakes . . . The telephone rings, voices chattering, the sound of feet walking along the path, tinkling of dropped glass. Then it's lunch time. Silence on the site as they leave for lunch.

KEVIN PADGHAM (AGE 8)

Talk about the design of houses and how they change over the years as new features are incorporated. Most houses now have central heating whereas it would have been usual to find houses being heated by coal fires or electric fires not so long ago. Do the children know anything about solar heating? Perhaps there is a house nearby where solar panels are visible in the roof. This, of course, is a recent development in the search for efficient ways of conserving energy. Can the children think of how they could be less wasteful with energy sources in their homes — turning off lights, turning down heat, wearing an extra layer of clothes etc? Discuss measures that are taken to help conserve energy within the home — double glazing, loft insulation, cavity walls. Have any children got these in their homes? Can they explain how they work?

Suggest that children think about their own homes. What can they see from their bedroom windows? Read Ian Souter's poem and ask children to listen for things that the poet saw or heard, then make a similar list which could be turned into a poem that also begins, *From my window I see . . .*

From My Window

From my window I see,
the lonely tree at the bottom of our garden
waving to catch my attention.
"Come and look, come and look,"
its long fingers seem to be saying
But I'm drawn upwards,
off towards black lumps of cloud
that swagger into view
as if they were chasing trouble.

"Move over sun, your time's up,"
they appear to announce
as daylight suffers a short power loss.
Down on the streets cars are playing,
'Now you see me, now you don't'
behind neighbouring houses,
while on the distant skyline
a train rushes along chattering,
"Mustn't be late, mustn't be late!"

IAN SOUTER

Similarly think about what can be seen or heard at night or at a different time of year. Draw up another list. How does this compare with the first list? Those children who so wish might attempt a second poem. (With such an exercise as this, younger children can, of course, interpret their ideas pictorially. Day and Night or Summer and Winter drawings might be juxtaposed and captioned.)

Ask the children what they like or dislike about where they live. They will probably hold quite strong views. A large proportion of seven and eight year olds at St Leonard's C.E. School told me that they didn't like where they lived and gave me a number of reasons — no garden, on a main road, buses and other traffic stop me getting to sleep, only a balcony to play on, garden is hilly, noise of the next door neighbour who is a builder. I asked if improvements could be made that might persuade the children to change their minds. Most children wanted somewhere to play so that they didn't have to play in the street. Some wanted flatter gardens so they could play ball games.

Talk about the sort of gardens that children would like. What features would be included? Suggest that they draw rough plans of their own gardens showing how they could improve them or alternatively, draw up plans for an ideal garden. How much of the garden would be grass? Would there be a patio, pond, barbecue area, swing, sand pit etc?

Suggest that children think about being explorers in their gardens. Work as a class to begin with and look at gardens in an imaginative way, as did six and seven year olds at Cuxton Infant School in Kent:

Exploring the World of My Garden

I explored my garden and I tiptoed across the desert
(that's the sand pit.)
I was strangled by a boa constrictor
(that's a worm.)
The swamp dragged me down
(that's the mud.)
A tiger creeps through the jungle
(that's my cat in the long grass.)
The lake is full of crocodiles
(they're the fish that open their mouths.)
A wolf is howling loudly
(that's my dog barking at me.)

RANSCOMBE CLASS POEM

Talk about the streets where children live. What do they like and dislike about them? How could they be improved? Five and six year olds at Bexhill Down Infants school were quite certain what their streets needed — a café (Macdonalds), tables and chairs, a play area, a sweet shop, a toy shop and so on. I asked if these 'improvements' would suit everyone. What about old people, what changes would they like to see? The children agreed that tables and chairs would be helpful when an elderly person needed a rest. They also thought that there should be a dress shop, a market, book shop, music, flowers and trees.

Read the children Anatol Sleeman's description of the street where he lives. Ask them to listen while you read it twice. Tell them that you will want to know what they can remember about the street when you have finished. Pick out the important points. It is a busy street, noisy, many juggernauts, large buildings, a wide street etc. Can the children write about their own streets in a similar way? What makes them interesting? Are there interesting characters and people in their streets — shopkeepers, noisy or nosey neighbours, people going to work, dustmen, window cleaners etc? Such an activity can help to reinforce the idea of place, where children live, how they interact with others and how others interact within the street.

Our Street

Our street is quite busy, heavy traffic, including foreign juggernauts pass almost continuously on their way to the M4 motorway, and cause a lot of noise and pollution. Many windows in our street bear stickers reading 'Ban the juggernauts'.

The houses in our street are four storey Victorian buildings, some of which are cared for and others which are derelict and even have squatters in.

Gunter Grove is fairly windy because it is a wide street running from north to south. Often I can see television aerials hanging lopsidedly on the rooftops.

The summer sun encourages quantities of little flowers whose colours brighten up the front gardens. A mature lime tree as tall as the houses showers our garden and paths with sticky green leaves, which annoy my father when he parks his shiny black car underneath. The street is wide enough to have one lane of parked cars and two others moving in the same direction. The pile of rubble on the pavement marks the place where the Gas Board men installed pipes that supply our house with hot water. They abandoned us saying they would be back in thirty minutes and leaving their tools behind. We haven't heard from them since. Gunter Grove is one of the places where Concorde can be seen in its final descent to Heathrow Airport.

ANATOL SLEEMAN (AGE 8) YOUNG WRITERS 1984 (HEINEMANN)

Do any children live in streets that are similar to Anatol's? If not, how do their streets differ? Are any children familiar with Neighbourhood Watch schemes? Explain how the schemes operate or perhaps persuade the chairperson of a local group or a policeman to come and talk to the children. Emphasise that such schemes draw people together and promote the notion of 'looking out' for each other. Are there other ways in which people in the same street or neighbourhood can meet others and forge the sort of links that foster a spirit of togetherness? Perhaps there could be a similar scheme to Neighbourhood Watch where everyone would concern themselves with the environment and whether its best interests were being served. Consideration would be given to the needs of the area — its inhabitants, buildings and wildlife.

How do the streets look at different times of day, or at different times of year? How do they look when it's raining, or when snow has fallen overnight? How do they look on a blazing hot day in summer? Is there something special about where you live on Guy Fawkes Night? Are there different smells and sounds?

Wes Magee writes about taking a walk on a snowy Christmas day:

Christmas Day Walk

Down to the end
of our housing estate,
across fields
to Hanging Man's Wood
where skeleton trees
stand black and bare
and the chilled air
freezes your blood.

In Wellington boots
we crunch through the snow,
watch a magpie
flutter and squawk.
A fluffed-up thrush
trembles on a thin twig
and the sky is grey
as wet chalk.

At the edge of the wood
we stand stone-still
as moth snowflakes
start to whirl down.
There are no cars on the roads.
not a sound
as Christmas Day
blankets the town.

WES MAGEE

Talk about the poem. Note how the poet writes of 'Hanging Man's Wood'. This is probably a local name, are there similar places that the children know about? Why is the sky *'grey as wet chalk'?* What about *'moth snowflakes'?* Why do we talk of a blanket of snow?

As a class, choose a time of year to write about and gather different impressions of what it is like. Suggest that children close their eyes and take an imaginary walk down the street where they live. Where does it lead, who do you meet and what do you see and hear? Children should present this as a poem or a piece of prose, and try to include some local detail.

Younger or less able children might care to draw their street at different times of the day or year and to caption each picture.

There may be children in the class who are less familiar with the area because they are new arrivals. They may prefer to think about the place where they lived previously. They will have particular insights to offer when talking about moving house. They will know what it is like to pack up at their old house, to leave behind familiar surroundings, to travel to a new area, to unpack and to look out onto a different street. They will have faced the challenges of a new school and making new friends.

Perhaps some of the children who have experienced a house move will be willing to talk about what it was like. Other children might work out a list of questions to ask them: What did you miss most about your old house? Were you worried about moving? What was good about your new home?

Gareth Owen writes about leaving home and focuses on a number of small but important details. His writing helps us to understand that moving house is an emotional as well as a physical upheaval:

Leaving Home
House looks right different with no furniture in. All echoey. Like a church. I keep thinking. What does the house feel like. Being left behind. I know a house can't *feel* but you can't help wondering. Get this feeling that it knows it's being left behind. Keep getting this feeling that it knows we're going somewhere we think is better. I keep thinking we should be taking it with us like the cat and the budgie. Hope it knows somehow I don't want to go. I'd like it to know that.

People are different. Dad went all round to have a last look. Like an official goodbye. Mam wouldn't. Just busy with bags and things. Straight in the car. She won't even look round when we leave. I want to fix it. Like the last moment. Remember it like that.

Keep thinking about the things I won't see again. Like where I did that crayon of a gnome on the bathroom wallpaper. Mam went mad. Was only five. "What's that?" she shouted. "Snow White". I always thought Snow White was a gnome. And where the paint looks like a hippopotamus laughing. Used to look at it when I was in the bath.

Hippopotamus laughing. Nobody else could see it except me.

'What hippopotamus?'

'Look there's its ear; there's its eye. See it laugh.'

'This one does.'

I could see it alright.

What about the people who come after? Won't mean anything to them. They'll paper over the gnome called Snow White. And there'll be my hippo laughing away and nobody'll see him.

Know all these places. Greenfield Road, Halifax Road, Sandringham Crescent, Grosvenor Avenue. Feel they belong to me. All these streets. Where I had that fight with Barry Cross. Where Andy fell off his bike and the bread van ran over his fixed wheel. And Dad belted him. Where Harry Barton's dog got run over and only has three legs. Know all these places.

One place I had to go . . . this one special place at the bottom of our garden. It's like a den made out of old tyres and planks and corrugated iron, next to the compost heap. It's where I'd go if I came home and nobody was in. Or if I'd had a row with somebody. Always used to go there. Before the car left went there on me own. Sat in the black dark there. Smells of tea leaves and cabbage but I liked it. Wanted to stay there for ever. Could hear Mam shouting at me. It was funny, I could . . . like . . . I wanted to say where I was but my voice wouldn't let me.

In the end my body got up and went. Mam asked me where I'd been hiding myself, but I could tell she wasn't really mad . . . that she knew . . . I didn't want to talk.

I just got in the car and we drove off. Something . . . I had a feeling something was ending. It was like there was two of me. I was in the car, I could still sort of see myself at the bottom of the garden.

It was like I was leaving myself behind.

GARETH OWEN

Read Gareth Owen's account to the children. Can they tell you some of the special things that he was upset to be leaving behind? There are lots of special places with special memories.

The children's own writing might revolve around a repeating phrase: *When I left my house, I missed . . .* or alternatively, if children haven't experienced a house move, *If I left my house I'd remember . . .* Emphasise that Mum, Dad, brothers, sisters, and the family pets will all be going to the new house and try to help them focus on the small details that make a house and its surroundings special. Perhaps, like Gareth Owen, it is a camp or den in the garden or maybe some other special place. Perhaps there's a creaky stair, a squeaking door, a cupboard where you hide, a shelf where you bang your head, strange noises from the central heating or a tree in the garden that you climb. Think too, about things that have happened at your house.

James sets his poem out like this:

If I left my house
I'd remember the times
that I climbed on the garage roof
from my bedroom window
and seeing my grandma's house
over the road.

If I left my house
I'd remember my bedroom
next to the stairs
and the big trees that lean
over Saltcote Lane.

If I left my house
I'd remember the big lump
that I went over on my bike
and the muddy patch
where I play football.

JAMES TREE (AGE 8)

Children might enjoy writing further about a very special place:

My favourite place is in front of the Arga. I like it because it warms my bottom when I lean against it.

JESSICA HIBBERT (AGE 8)

My Special Place

My special place is
Downstairs,
In the hall.
A room,
Well not so much of a room,
Because it's kind of chopped off.
It's the room
where I work
On my own,
Writing or
Typing or on the computer.
My silent special place.

JESSIE ECCLES (AGE 8)

Older children could be told something about evacuation during World War Two. Encourage empathy between themselves and the children who were sent away, not knowing whether they would ever see their homes or families again. There are several books containing the evacuees' own accounts of what it was like and these would be worth searching out for material at an appropriate level. (Two of the best are *No Time to Wave Goodbye: True Stories of Britain's 3,500,000 Evacuees* by Ben Wicks, Bloomsbury 1988, and *Children of the Blitz: Memories of Wartime Childhood* by Robert Westall, Viking 1985/Penguin 1987.)

Ask if anyone has ever slept in a tent? Can they say what it was like? It was probably in the summer when the nights were reasonably warm. Has anyone ever tried to construct a camp in the woods or in a garden? What materials were used? What were the problems? Would it have been possible to sleep inside it?

Talk about feeling cold. In what situations have children ever felt really cold? Imagine what it would be like to sleep in a tent or a homemade camp on a night when temperatures fall to below freezing.

Ask the children what being homeless really means. Has anyone seen homeless people pictured or interviewed on the TV? Why were they homeless? What conditions were they living in? Explain to the children that many people in our cities are 'sleeping rough', in doorways, on benches or in cardboard shelters, not just in the summer months but on freezing cold nights in winter too. Attempt some sort of empathy through drama. An interviewer talks to a homeless person — where have you come from, why are you here, where will you be sleeping tonight, how do you feel about that, is there anything that can be done about it?

Suggest that children in groups design a shelter that they would possibly be able to sleep in, using throwaway materials such as boxes, sheets of cardboard, cloth, newspapers. Then assemble everything and have a go at making the shelter. What problems are they likely to face?

When the shelter is built to the children's satisfaction, ask them to draw up a step-by-step plan to show how it was built and how problems can be avoided. Spend some time in the shelter and imagine sleeping there on a cold night. Some children might like to write about an imagined night in the open, perhaps in the form of an hour-by-hour commentary on what happened and how they felt.

What can be done to help solve the problems of homeless people — has anyone any ideas?

Try to find pictures of shanty towns or feeding camps. Talk about the pictures. Why are all these people without proper homes? Explain how some people are forced to leave their homes because there is no food for their families. They then travel many miles to feeding camps where some food is available. Sometimes such a journey involves crossing the border into another country. Introduce the word 'refugee' to older children. Bernard Ashley's book *Boat Girl* (Julia MacRae — Redwings 1990) might help seven and eight year olds to understand what it means to leave your own country and settle in another. In Ashley's book, Kim Lung, the Vietnamese girl from Dockside School relives her escape from Vietnam whilst involved in a game of hide and seek on a week's school visit to Wales.

Reading Resources

Poetry

Down Our Street by Jennifer and Graeme Curry (Methuen 1988). An entertaining collection of poems that explore the street and its many moods — from street parties to break-ins, street cats to new cars.

Salford Road (Young Lions 1988) and *Song of the City* (Fontana Lions 1985) both by Gareth Owen. Some poems suitable, particularly 'Salford Road' from the former and 'The New House' from the latter.

'The Building Site' by Marian Lines and 'House' by Leonard Clark, both included in *A First Poetry Book* ed. John Foster OUP 1979.

The Young Puffin Book of Verse ed. Barbara Ireson (Puffin). Section on 'Homes and Houses'.

Fiction

Christmas In Exeter Street by Diana Hendry (Julia MacRae Books 1989). Delightful account of how the house accommodates large numbers of guests, both expected and unexpected on Christmas Eve.

Moving Gives Me a Stomach Ache by Heather McKend and Heather Collins (OUP 1988). A young boy is reluctant to leave his house and can only think of everything he will be leaving behind.

Moving House by Nicky Daw (A. & C. Black 1987). Leaving friends, packing up, loading the van, the new house, new school. Fiction plus information.

Moving Molly by Shirley Hughes (Picture Lions). When Molly's family move house there isn't a lot to do in her new home at first, but soon she begins to explore and finds that life isn't so dull after all.

The Big Concrete Lorry by Shirley Hughes (Walker Books 1989). The Pattersons need more space for their growing family and decide to build an extension to their home. Neighours rally round to help when wet concrete is delivered unexpectedly.

Non-fiction

Homes by John Foster (Hodder and Stoughton 1990). A look at the development of housing in the twentieth century. Good quotes — what it's like to live in tower blocks, on new estates etc.

Houses and Homes and *Building a House* (Mary Glasgow Publications Ltd. 1990). Topic Support packs — lots of material for developing skills etc.

Look Around: The Street by Clive Pace and Jean Birch (Wayland 1988). Lots of ideas for finding out details about 'street furniture' — barriers and bollards, telephone boxes, post boxes, markings and signs etc.

For a comprehensive listing of books on *House and Home* consult *Books For Keeps* No. 51, July 1988.

The School

HOW do children travel to school? Hold a class survey to see who walks, who comes by car or by some other method. In Stanley Cook's poem *'Walking to School'*, we walk with him while he records what he sees as he passes by various houses. Read the poem to the children and ask them to listen out for things that the poet sees and creatures he meets:

Walking To School

This is the road down which I go
Early to school every day
And these are the houses on the way
Parading in a long straight row.

This is the house of the motoring man
And the car he is mending sits
Without its wheels on piles of bricks
And he's taken the engine out of his van.

This is the house with a big wide drive
With a friendly retriever
Who wags his tail to greet you
And comes to the road to watch you arrive.

This is the house you can hardly see
Among so many lofty trees
That rise in the air like fountains of leaves
And who lives there's a mystery to me.

This is the house my friend lives in:
If he sees me coming he'll wait

Hiding behind his garden gate
And try to frighten me out of my skin.

This is the wooden bungalow
Where a seagull far from the sea
Calls from his perch on top of the chimney
And scolds the people down below.

This is the house with the rocky pool,
A little windmill, a wooden bridge
And a gnome who fishes at the water's edge
And here next to it is the gate to school.

STANLEY COOK

Suggest that the children choose a verse from the poem and illustrate it, making sure that they include everything that the poet writes about in that verse.

Talk about the routes that children take to school. Can anyone tell the class about his or her journey to school? Think about the roads you travel along, whether on foot or by car, and the buildings that you pass by. Try to group together children who travel the same route so that they can discuss what they see and hear each day. Make up lists of observations or questions that could lead to a class survey. How many children pass by a particular parade of shops? How many pass the fire station, how many cross at the school crossing point?

Five and six year olds at Bexhill Down Infants listed a playground with swings, slides and a climbing frame, squirrels in the trees, a dead hedgehog, two dogs — Susie and Bonzo, cats, magpies, bread on the ground, a fire station, fire engine, post office and a cafe. They heard distant trains, an ambulance, birds, the sea, friends calling, seagulls, children playing and a police car. They also produced a smells list — breakfast smell at the café, petrol, flowers, cooking, smoke, and a school smell.

Some of these lists might feature on maps of the local area. The places where children smell distinctive smells could be marked on the map, colour coded and then commented on — at the junction of these two streets we can smell bacon and eggs cooking, we smell petrol as we pass by the filling station, and so on. This could lead to the writing of trails for other children to follow — a noisy trail, a smelly trail etc.

Ask the children whether there would be similar items on a list of sights, sounds and smells for the journey home from school. One six year old informed me that the fish and chip shop was open then. Some children might like to write about their journey home:

Things I see on my way home

When I come out of school I see the school bus waiting. I rush in case I miss it — wallop, crash, up the rickety rackety steps. We go past all the houses. I see sparkling fields with sheep in the sun. In five minutes time I look out of the window and we are going past the lake, past the men playing golf on the golf course. Home at last, I get off the bus and walk down the lane.

SARA BENNETT (AGE 7)

Children could consider whether improvements might be made along the route that they take to school. Perhaps a busy road needs a subway, a footbridge, or a new pedestrian crossing. Are the pavements extra narrow at one point ? Are the paving stones damaged and likely to cause accidents? Think about the needs of disabled people or babies in pushchairs.

Older children might attempt to give directions from home to school with the aid of street maps. Alternatively they could make up a network of roads, name them, and mark any important buildings, then give the map a key. Directions could then be given for another child to follow. Pairs of children would then check each other's accuracy and decide whether the directions could be written in a more helpful way. Simon might have improved his example by pointing out the railway line at the end of Rear Road, the green on his left in Up Street and the car park in Join Road. He could have concluded by saying that the Sad Street school is on the right, opposite the green.

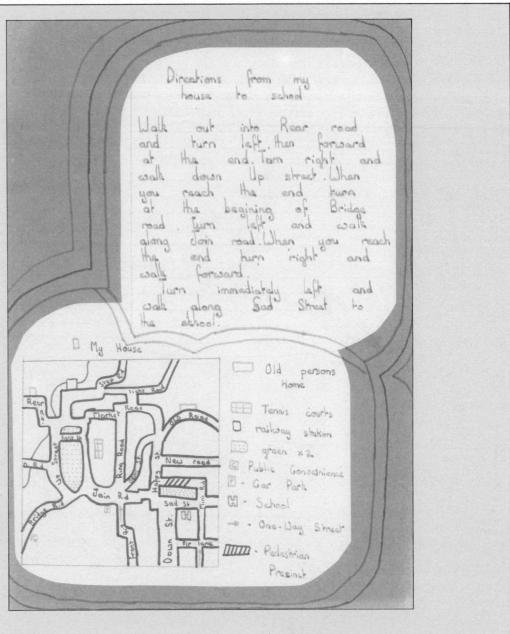

SIMON HARRIS (AGE 8)

What happens in the school playground? Go through the senses and ask for ideas. Brainstorm a list of activities for each sense and write them yourself on large sheets of paper or on the board. Children could then be asked to include ideas from these lists in their own writing about the playground:

> The playground looks like a snooker table because children knock into each other and drop down . . . The children are very much like hungry fish in a green sea with the benches as boats.
>
> CAROLINE FULLER (AGE 7)

Read the children Stanley Cook's *'In the Playground'*. Ask them to listen and then pick out everything that is happening in the poem. Talk about the playground at different times of the year. Younger children might like to illustrate a line from the poem: *'In Winter I glide/ Along the slide'* or *'When falling leaves come dodging down/We catch them before they reach the ground.'* Alternatively a class collage could be put together, either showing the playground as a mêlée of activity, or in four sections depicting seasonal differences. Can the children then think of questions to write out and place round the collage so that other children can look at the picture and try to find the right answers?

In the Playground

In the playground the railings are green,
Too narrow to put your head between
And there I skip like a bouncing ball
Or bounce my ball upon the wall.
When it rains the puddles are fun
To test the toes of my wellingtons.
When falling leaves come dodging down
We catch them before they reach the ground.
In Winter I glide
Along the slide
And snowballs make
My fingers ache.
In the playground
Some run round,
Some walk
And talk,
Some stand
on their hands
Against a wall
And some do nothing at all

STANLEY COOK

Stanley Cook's poem ends with the line *'And some do nothing at all.'* Perhaps these children don't enjoy playtime for one reason or another. Think about the layout of playgrounds. Perhaps there should be different areas in the playground — a quiet area, an area for games activities, a play and exercise area with logs, tubes, a climbing frame etc. Consider how children can ensure that playtime is an enjoyable experience for everyone through consideration of other children's needs. Games players are sometimes thoughtless, knocking over smaller children in their haste to retrieve a ball. Some children are deliberately left out of games — 'We don't want Jean in our team.' Is this fair? How do those who are left out feel about the situation? List ways of persuading children to join in with group activities.

Playground activity is a good source of inspiration for improvisational drama. It is better for less experienced children to work in pairs as larger numbers can easily become somewhat confusing. Decide who the two characters are and what has happened. Perhaps there has been a fight and two children are arguing over whose fault it was. Perhaps two mums are talking when they meet in the morning, or two children are being unkind about a third child. Ensure that the children understand the situation and ask for suggestions from the rest of the class as to what might happen next. Those watching can help by saying what they liked about the piece of drama or by offering constructive criticism. 'I didn't like what they did because it was rubbish' is not acceptable whereas 'I didn't like what they did because they didn't concentrate' would be a valuable response.

Younger children will be keen to share memories of playschool and at some stage in their first school year it will be useful to think about the skills that they have acquired since starting school. 'What couldn't you do before you started school?' will help children to understand that all learning is developmental. Also ask, 'What do you expect to be able to do next year?' Seven and eight year olds will be able to look back on the first day or week at school and try to remember how they felt.

Starting School by Janet and Allan Ahlberg (Viking Kestrel 1988) is an absolute gem of a book and one that is a must for all young children to hear in their first term. It serves as a delightful introduction to school life and rings true with every page. It follows the progress of *'Gavin and Errol and Sophie and Sushma and David and Kate and Robert and Alison . . .'* as they experience school life for the first time. It will serve as first-rate stimulus material for the children's own sentence-making concerning the school environment.

It will also be valuable for younger children to learn that a school doesn't just consist of the teachers and dinner ladies. Make a list of everyone who works in school in one capacity or another — cook, canteen assistants, caretaker, cleaners, school secretary, 'lollipop lady' or man, mums and dads who help out in classrooms, plus the people who visit the school to help out in some way — nurse, doctor, dentist, police liaison officer etc. Perhaps some of these people can be persuaded to come to the classroom and talk about what they do to help in the running of the school.

Consider the school grounds and how effectively they are being used. Begin by making a list of everything children can think of within the school environs — the building itself, playgrounds, space for car-parking, sheds, swimming pool, football pitch, flowerbeds, trees etc. Can the children think of any other ways in which the grounds could be used? What about little-used areas? Are there already established nature areas — a pond, a bird table, a patch of uncut grass, a spinney, a vegetable garden, a rockery and so on? Can something be set up to improve the school environment?

Once a decision has been taken to set up a school garden, for example, children can keep diaries that record the progress of their work on the project. Photographs could be taken that show the chosen area prior to any work being done and the children could record their thoughts on the way it looks. Diary entries can be daily or weekly, compiled individually or written for a class book. In city schools where space is limited there is no reason why diaries cannot be written to record the planting of bulbs in pots or a window box and their progress observed and noted. Additional material might include notes on plants in general.

At Kingsmead C.P. School in Canterbury, Lesley Pearson informed her class of eight and nine year olds that there was a plan to build a chocolate factory on the school grounds.

The children wrote a report of the committee of enquiry into the proposal and then spoke at a meeting:

On Wednesday 20th June there was an enquiry in the State Hall.

First of all the committee called upon the 'For the Chocolate Factory to be built' group. The managers of the factory spoke first. They said that the school field was a big place to build the factory on and that tourists would come and buy their chocolate.

Next spoke the future workers who said that they had been out of work for a long time and had been promised jobs.

Next spoke the school department man who said that he wanted to sell the land because he needed profit for the teachers' pay.

Then the shop owners spoke and said it would be a good idea because they would sell the chocolate for them.

Then the people against spoke.

The teachers said it would not be a good idea because the children would not be able to hear the teachers speak. Another teacher said they would not be able to teach sport. A third teacher said that she didn't think it would be a good idea because the children wouldn't be able to study wildlife.

Next spoke the children who said that they would not be able to hear their teacher speak. Another child said that he usually went the short way home across the school field but if they build the chocolate factory then he'd have to go round the long way.

Then the environmentalists spoke and said that it would destroy the wildlife and pollute the river.

LAURA DRAY (AGE 9)

Some children then wrote newspaper reports:

SCHOOL STRANDED WITH NOWHERE TO PLAY

Why should the school lose their field? They need their field to survive. If this chocolate factory is built it will kill wildlife and children will not be able to do animal investigations. They are desperately trying to get it back. If you have any ideas to save the school field phone 462360 and tell the school.

NICKY FRENCH (AGE 9)

What do children know about school life in other countries? Individual or group research could be undertaken and knowledge assembled and shared. This would be a good moment to emphasise library skills. Where do you find books on countries in the school library? How do you find out if the book contains a section on schools? How do you use encyclopaedias, and how do you decide which bits of information are important?

Look at schools in countries such as China, India and Nepal, in Arab countries such as Egypt, Libya, Morocco and Tunisia, and in African countries such as Nigeria and Kenya. Where do children learn, what do they learn, how many children are taught in each class and at what age they leave school and start work.

Letters could be written to appropriate foreign embassies or tourist information boards seeking more information about school life. Perhaps it can be arranged for children to actually write to children in foreign schools so that they can learn about each other's lives.

School Links International: A New Approach to Primary School Linking Around the World by Rex Beddis and Cherry Mares (Avon County Council/Tidy Britain Group Schools Research Project 1988) explains how children and their classes can be linked up worldwide. It is worth reprinting the aims of class-to-class linking from SLI:

To encourage and help pupils develop a knowledge and understanding of themselves, their families and friends, their local neighbourhood and environment, and their country using a wide range of study methods.

To encourage and help pupils communicate to others this understanding of themselves, their community, environment and country, and their feelings and attitudes towards them . . .

To enable pupils to learn something of people, neighbourhoods, environments and ways of life in other parts of the world through the receipt and active study of similar communications from pupils of their own age.

Through this deeper understanding to counteract prejudice, develop sympathetic and caring attitudes to other people and ways of life, and a sense of responsibility for the environment, both locally and globally.

SLI stresses that materials should be selected from normal class work and that the first exchanges will inevitably contain much about the pupils and their personal interests. Children also enjoy finding out similarities and differences between their own schools and those of children in other parts of the world. They can swap news of the special events that take place in their schools and either through words or a series of pictures, relate to each other the pattern of their daily timetables.

Very young children can work on captioned pictures that show something of their life at school and of the many people who work in the school community.

Reading Resources

Poetry

Please Mrs Butler (Kestrel 1983/Puffin 1984) and *Heard it in the Playground* (Viking Kestrel 1989/Puffin 1990) both by Allan Ahlberg. The former is probably the most popular book of poetry in schools today while the latter is almost as good. Try 'Dog in the Playground' from *Please Mrs Butler* if you've had a bad day!

School's Out compiled by John Foster (OUP 1988). A wonderful collection with poems on almost every aspect of school life. Many will be suitable for 7 and 8 year olds.

The Dragon on the Wall and other poems by Stanley Cook (Blackie 1989). A number of school poems including 'Mr Fitzsimmons' — the school caretaker.

The Witch's Brew and other poems by Wes Magee (CUP 1989). Lots of poems about school including 'An A-Z of items found on the school roof by the caretaker.'

You'll Love That Stuff: Poems from many cultures selected by Morag Styles (CUP 1986). Section 'At School Today' allows us a glimpse of school life in other countries.

Fiction

Boat Girl by Bernard Ashley (Julia MacRae — Redwings 1990). How Kim, a Vietnamese girl, copes with the school week in Wales.

My New School by Neil and Ting Morris (Macdonald 1988). Beth is apprehensive about starting at her new school. Plenty of positive experiences soon reassure her.

Starting School by Fiona Pragoff — Story by Peter Heaslip — (Methuen 1986/Magnet 1988). A photographic record of Lucy's first day at school.

The School Cat by Anne Managan (Hodder & Stoughton — Hedgehogs 1990). An 'easy reader', one step up from picture books. How Fred the kitten is adopted as the school cat.

The School Outing by Diana Bentley (Wayland 1988). This focuses on an outing to a farm in Essex. Lots of good photographs. Also in the same series, *The Class Teacher, The Dinner Ladies, The Lollipop Man, The Road Safety Officer, The School Caretaker, The School Fete, The School Secretary.*

The School Trip by Nick Buterworth and Mick Inkpen (Hodder and Stoughton 1990). A gem. Read it prior to any trip, particularly a museum visit.

Non-fiction

Penfriends by Heidi Larson (A. & C. Black 1990). A London school exchanges letters with one in Bournemouth. Now Seema and Carly are about to meet. A photographic record of their day.

Round the World: Learning (The Save the Children Fund and Macmillan Education 1981). Children growing up around the world, their schools, health, customs and games.

Schools by Judith Crosher (Hodder and Stoughton 1989). A look at schools and school life during the twentieth century, including different kinds of schools — for circus children, canal children, theatre children etc.

What Can I See? In the Playground by Cecilia Fitzsimons (Hamish Hamilton 1990). One of a series of picture books for the very young introducing children, in this instance, to the school playground, and the range of plants and creatures that they may see there.

Towns and Cities

I Live in the City

I live in the city, yes I do,
I live in the city, yes I do,
I live in the city, yes I do,
Made by human hands.

Black hands, white hands, yellow and brown
All together built this town.
Black hands, white hands, yellow and brown
All together the wheels go round.

Black hands brown hands, yellow and white
Built the buildings tall and bright,
Black hands brown hands, yellow and white
Filled them all with shining light.

Black hands, white hands, brown and tan
Milled the flour and cleaned the pan,
Black hands, white hands, brown and tan —
The working woman and the working man.

I live in the city, yes I do,
I live in the city, yes I do,
I live in the city, yes I do,
Made by human hands.

ANONYMOUS, U.S.A.

IF CHILDREN live away from large cities ask if anyone has ever been to London or to another big city. How did they feel about it? What can children tell the class about their trip to a city?

Read the above poem. Children should pick this up fairly quickly themselves and by the second reading will probably be joining in. Suggest that small groups might like to learn different verses so that the poem could be recited to other classes at an assembly that looks at city life. Ask whether they feel that the writer likes living in the city. Talk about different races building the city and working there together, with everyone making the most of his or her talents. Discuss the idea of community — whether in towns and cities or at school — where we try to care about each other. Help promote a positive view with the aid of further poems/songs such as *Black and White, The Family of Man* and *When I needed a neighbour.*

Whether they live in cities and towns or elsewhere, children will be able to think of words and phrases to describe how they feel about being in a city. Suggest that children in groups compile their own lists and then report back to the class. Ask them to try to think of words and ideas that no one else will have thought of. Afterwards, write the words onto large sheets of paper to act as a wordstore for any future writing on the subject.

Talk about the different people who work in our towns and cities, and the different services they help to run — shops, banks and building societies, estate agents, offices, transport, road repairs, sewers etc. If the children were to work in a city what job would they want to do? Younger children could draw a picture of a taxi driver, a nurse, a secretary or whatever and write a comment to go with it.

Consider the range of shops to be found in our towns and cities. Children could list these and perhaps draw a shop front, either from memory or from a sketch that was made on a visit to a shopping area. These could be arranged into a street collage. Decide on the name of the street.

Talk about the advantages of supermakets. Carry out a class survey to discover which ones are the most popular with children and their parents. What are superstores? How often do children visit D.I.Y. superstores or garden centres? What do their parents buy there?

Many cities have shopping centres where traffic is banned or indoor shopping areas. Do the children like visiting these? What are the advantages of such centres. What sort of shops do you usually find there? Older children might care to plan their ideal shopping centre and then annotate the plan to show what services are included.

Many shops sell goods from other countries. If possible, interview a greengrocer as to where his fruit originates. Find the countries mentioned and label them on a large wall map of the world. What is a delicatessen? Much of the food sold here will be from foreign countries. Can children bring to school any food labels and packaging that indicates that the contents came from another country? These could also be pinned up around the map and linked to their countries of origin by wool or thread. Are there shops that sell clothes from other countries? Are there restaurants that offer food from India or China, or from European countries such as Italy or Greece?

From quite an early age, children will identify with the models that they make and a model in the classroom can be the starting point for imaginative development along a number of lines. Young children will enjoy making model houses from boxes and no matter the degree of sophistication, when these models are assembled together they will suffice as a street. With two or more classes contributing to the same model it should be possible to build a small town. Older children will demand greater realism and be able to widen the scope of buildings to include shops, cinema, school, church, town hall, police station, fire station etc. All these will, of course, stem from suggestions that the children make concerning the variety of buildings to be found in towns and cities.

The model town can be extended in whatever way you wish. Model vehicles can be added along with telephone boxes, post boxes, street signs and so on. Gardens could be laid out plus some fields at the edge of the town. Perhaps there is a market or a children's playground.

Suggest then, that the children try to bring the town to life. Who lives in the houses, where do they shop, where do they work? Some children might care to work on an edition of the town newspaper, others might write diary entries for the people who live in the houses.

Seven and eight year old children at Hollington Junior School in Hastings, developed their own town which they named Foreston, as the town itself was surrounded by forests. They thought up laws and rules for the inhabitants of Foreston:

Foreston laws

No hunting.
No playing football in the streets
do not drop litter.
No Smashing glass.
No Cycling.
No vandalism.
No throwing stones.
Keep dogs on leads.
clear up dog mess.
No painting on wall.
Dont be nasty.
Dont Cut trees Down.
No Smoking.
No fighting.
Dont let stray dogs out.
Dont steal from shops.
No picking flowers
No drinking in the car.
No stealing birds eggs.

Their teacher then planted a letter from a building firm who wanted to cut down the forests so that the town might be extended. The children discussed the pros and cons of such an action.

Similar problems might be introduced. For example, tell the children that it has been decided to build a bypass road which will skirt the town and pass through nearby fields. Ask what will be the advantages and disadvantages of such a plan.

One seven year old at St Leonards School in Sussex was worried about plans for a new road close by his house. It would pass through a field where he played football with his friends. What could he do about it? Other children thought that he should speak to the council, 'phone them up or write a letter saying, *Please could you give us back our field because we play football there.* Someone else suggested that he should stand in the way when they tried to build the road!

A similar problem was presented to seven and eight year olds in Rye:

Dear Sir,

I disagree with you putting a motorway by our school. It will disturb us trying to work. The motorway will destroy the countryside. We would not be able to play in the park. Rye is a peaceful town. I do not want to see it destroyed please. At a late hour, when people are asleep, the noise would be terrible. The farmers will have to find a new place for sheep.

I object.

Yours faithfully,

GEMMA MILHAM (AGE 7)

Ask the children to consider the advantages of taking traffic away from towns — cleaner, quieter towns, less fumes, increased safety etc.

It would be interesting to explore such a situation through drama, having first made sure that children were acquainted with the arguments on both sides. What happens when the case is presented to a council official. How do the road builders react to people standing in the way of their bulldozers?

Read the children Charles Keeping's picture book *Adam and Paradise Island* (OUP 1989). In the story, Paradise Island is a small island in the middle of a muddy creek, linked to either side by stone bridges. There are lovely illustrations showing the shops and shopkeepers who trade on the island and of two former itinerants — Old Varda and Ma Burley who live there. To the council, Paradise Island is a mess and a decision is taken to build a fast toll road across the island linking both sides of the creek. Adam loves the island and is dismayed to see all the destruction taking place. However, while the road is being built, Adam and his friends, with the help of Old Varda and Ma Burley are busy salvaging an area of the island and turning it into a children's playground. At the conclusion of the story, almost everyone gets what they want.

A visit to a busy street would be a useful addition to work on towns and cities. If possible arrange a walk and ask children to concentrate on one particular aspect, in this instance noise.

Noises

Rubbish clunking into dustcarts,
Metal being blown across the road,
A train bumping over the track,
Tick, tack, clickety clack.
A revving noise as the car key turns,
A tinkling noise as the engine ticks on,
A clattering noise as the trucks chug past,
Chugging and crawling up the steep bumpy hill.
Feet banging on the ground,
Tap tap tap tap tapping away.

. . . .

MARK GRIFFITHS AND STEVEN LITTLEWOOD (AGE 8)

In the following poem, Ian Souter complains about noise:

Surrounded by Noise

I'm surrounded by noise,
LISTEN!

BEEP! BEEP! BEEP!
A car down on the street.
BOOGIE! BOOGIE! BOOGIE!
A disco beat.

THUMP! THUMP! THUMP!
A hammer next door.
THUD! THUD! THUD!
Brother jumping on the floor.

CLACKETY! CLACKETY! CLACKETY!
A train rattles by.
ROAR! ROAR! ROAR!
A plane climbs the sky.

DRILL! DRILL! DRILL!
A workman on the road.
NO! NO! NO!
Mum about to explode.

Everywhere, everything noisy and loud.
Isn't quietness in this world ever allowed!

IAN SOUTER

Children might like to have a go at writing in a similar way, either about noise in a town or city or about the noise in one particular place. Again, brainstorm for ideas first. If children wish they can use made-up spellings. Such pieces of writing are great fun when read aloud, preferably with a bit of practice in advance. If a tape recorder is handy then many children will find it less worrying to read their work into a microphone and listen to it later with everyone else. Ask other children whether they feel the various pieces really do make us think of the subject chosen by the writer.

Read Emma's poem to the children. Does she like London? Can they pick out the words and phrases that tell us how she feels — 'Busy, bustling streets', 'a dirty road', 'smoke and fumes', 'the commotion of people' etc.

London

Busy, bustling streets
Lined with people
And a dirty road
With smoke and fumes.
You try to get around
But you can't get anywhere.
In Summer you can't move
For the commotion of people
Rushing to get to work
Through the station.
But I don't really care
If they are late or early
As long as I am away
From all the fuss of London.

EMMA TAYLOR (AGE 8)

Emma writes of the 'smoke and fumes' of London. She has noticed that the air in a city has a different smell to Whitby air where she lives. She understands that the reason for this is the heavy traffic and the exhaust fumes that pollute the atmosphere. Tell the children about smog and how in many cities around the world, polluted air is trapped near the ground forming a poisonous fog. In cities such as Los Angeles and Tokyo, face masks are commonly seen being worn by cyclists who want to avoid breathing in too much badly polluted air.

One of the harmful substances in vehicle exhaust fumes is lead. Scientists have proved that breathing in too much lead may cause damage to the brain, particularly with young children. Ask the children if they know what has happened in recent years to try to ensure that there is less lead in the atmosphere? How many children have family cars that run on lead-free petrol? What colour tells us that petrol pumps contain unleaded fuel? Some children may care to design posters that try to persuade people to use unleaded fuel in their cars.

Can the children list forms of transport that don't pollute the air that we breathe? Consider too, other ways in which towns and cities might be improved for the benefit of those who live and work there. Perhaps there should be more pedestrian precincts where traffic is banned. Waste areas could be tidied up and turfed, or left as wild gardens (see *Sarah Scrap and Her Wonderful Heap* in the chapter on 'Waste and Recycling'). Mention how the parks and open spaces in London are considered to be 'the lungs of the city'. What do they think is meant by this? Perhaps brightly coloured murals might help to make built-up areas more attractive.

Young children will identify with Postman Pat as he pays a visit to London in *Postman Pat Goes to Town* by John Cunliffe (Hippo Books 1989). Pat is disturbed by the smoke and fumes, the hustle and bustle of thousands of people, and by the fear of getting lost. However he soon begins to appreciate the different experiences that are available in such cosmopolitan surroundings.

As Pat finds out in the above story, there are positive sides to city life. Many people enjoy living in urban areas for all sorts of reasons. Ask the children to think about the advantages — being close to sports and leisure centres, theatres, cinemas, a good range of eating places, shops and shopping complexes, medical facilities, a choice of schools, better public transport and so on. Compare these with the disadvantages of living in the countryside where transport services are irregular, small schools often struggle to prevent closure, and local shops can't compete with the big supermarkets.

Initiate a study of your nearest town or city. How long ago was it founded? What were the reasons that influenced the choice of site? Is it a market town or a centre that grew because of local industry? Were there important historical events that happened in the town or city? Where are the oldest buildings — what clues can they offer us? Are there any sites that are being redeveloped? — perhaps it would be possible to visit one. Has anything been learnt about the history of the area from the excavations? A town project might include the results of interviews with elderly residents who may well remember the way that the town looked when they were young.

Finally, consider the wildlife that inhabits our towns and cities. Dick King-Smith's *Town Watch: Look out for the wildlife in your town* (Puffin 1987) is packed with information about the many animals, birds and insects that make their homes among the buildings of our towns and cities. There are facts and anecdotes about the town fox, owls and bats, mice, badgers, hedgehogs, toads, bees, butterflies and so on, plus those creatures who scavenge rubbish tips and waste ground. Children will probably have their own observations to add and some detailed drawing and writing could result.

Reading Resources

Poetry

A Second Poetry Book complied by John Foster (OUP 1980) includes 'Town Fox' by Leonard Clark.

Poems for 7 year-olds and under chosen by Helen Nicoll (Kestrel 1983/Puffin 1984) including 'The Song the Train Sang' by Neil Adams, 'Building a Skyscraper' by James S. Tippett and 'Steam Shovel' by Charles Malam.

The Dragon on the Wall and other poems by Stanley Cook (Blackie 1989) including 'The Dustman', 'The Bulldozer', 'Television Aerials', The Fire Station' and 'The Bread Shop' among others.

The Howling Pandemonium and Other Noisy Poems, compiled by Zenka and Ian Woodward (Blackie 1990) including 'Death of the Steel Works' by Caroline Lamb.

The Squirrel in the Town and other nature poems by Stanley Cook (Blackie 1988) including the title poem plus others on urban wildlife.

Fiction

Goanna by Jenny Wagner (Viking Kestrel 1988). Goanna is a large Australian lizard whose way of life is threatened by the building of shops and offices.

Non-fiction

Earthwatch: Clean Air, Dirty Air by Lynne Patchett (A. & C. Black 1990). One of an excellent new series of environmental books. Fine for 7/8 year olds. Good section on traffic pollution.

Finding Out About: How Things Are Built by Helen Edom (Usborne Explainers 1989). Usual high quality from Usborne with simple explanations and cutaway illustrations to show how houses, skyscrapers, roads, bridges, tunnels and so on, are built.

Look Around: SHOPS by Clive Pace and Jean Birch (Wayland 1989). An attractive book, well set out with questions designed to set children thinking about all sorts of shops from mobiles to superstores, from kiosks to take-aways.

The Countryside

Mind that toad

There was a toad in the garden today.

He wasn't big, just a middle-sized, very handsome toad. His soft skin glistened yellow and brown among the nettles and scarlet poppies. His back legs looked impossibly fragile, spread out on the earth, and his toes (if toads have toes), long and delicate.

He must have wondered what I was doing there, prodding around and digging with the sharp-pronged garden fork. Both of us were surprised to see each other, and he looked at me with interest, or so I thought. His eyes were a beautiful amber, the colour of sun shining through brown glass. He was only there for a moment, hidden, shy, on his own.

That part of our garden is very wild and tangled with every sort of weed you can think of. I wanted to clear it and plant more spinach and lettuce, but after meeting that toad I couldn't. It was his, after all, that patch.

I felt like telling him I was sorry I'd disturbed him, and begging him not to go away. And everything I saw from then on could have been a toad. Glossy brown holly leaves, dropped in the hot July afternoon, could have been the toad. He might be under the bramble shoots or cool green ground elder that run untamed there. I kept thinking — Mind That Toad!

I put the garden fork back into the shed, and left him to himself.

ANN BONNER

READ Ann Bonner's account to the children. Talk about the toad that she discovered — his *'soft skin'* that *'glistened yellow and brown'*, his back legs *'impossibly fragile,'* his eyes *'the colour of sun shining through brown glass.'* Ask if the children have ever discovered small creatures in a similar way. Can anyone tell about what happened?

Why was Ann Bonner careful not to harm the toad? Introduce the word *Conservation.* Does anyone know what it means? Point out to the children that human beings are only a small part of our world, but that it is up to us to act responsibly towards the creatures and plants that share it with us. Again ask for the children's own anecdotes — has anyone helped to save the life of a small creature? This is a good moment to talk about insects and spiders that many children kill without a second thought. What gives us the right to end their lives?

Children might like to produce two captioned pictures side by side showing right and wrong ways of relating to wildlife.

Seven and eight year olds will enjoy listening to *The Boy and the Swan* by Catherine Storr (Andre Deutsch 1987). This story concerns a lonely boy who lives with his deaf grandmother in an area of flat marshland. One day he discovers a pair of wild swans and watches them regularly. However, the swans die from lead poisoning but the boy saves one of their eggs and cares for it until it hatches into a cygnet. The story shows us how the actions of an individual ensured that a wild creature survived and returned to the wild.

Two excellent reference books for five and six year olds are written by Cecilia Fitzsimons and published by Hamish Hamilton in the *What Can I See? series*. These are *In the Field* and *In the Woods*. Both books introduce children to the range of plants and animals that live in these habitats and can lead to further investigation into particular interests. Observations can be made about different creatures and word banks built up to enable young children to write simple poems. In this instance, Lisa writes a 'before' and 'after' poem:

Metamorphosis

Caterpillars are green
And fat
They are soft
Hungry
Long creepy wriggly
Crawly
Small and big.

Butterflies are symmetrical
They are fluttery
Pretty
Beautiful coloured
Delicate, thin
Soft patterned and silky.

LISA POTTS (AGE 6)

Children may enjoy thinking about the following poem in which each verse is a riddle concerning an animal. When they have guessed these four, they might like to try writing their own. Suggest that they keep the lines short and that they attempt to rhyme in this instance.

Hidden Creatures

Fat body,
Curly tail,
Eating swill,
From a pail.

Small squeak,
Long tail,
Little creature,
Very frail.

Bright eyes,
Bobbing rear,
Twitching whiskers,
Frozen fear.

Sharp spikes,
Black snout,
Spring's here,
Creeping out.

ANITA MARIE SACKETT

Sue Densem's class of five and six year olds at Christchurch School in St. Leonards-on-Sea spent some time thinking about hedgehogs and how they hibernated for the winter. They talked a lot about the places that hedgehogs chose for their sleeping quarters and the dangers that some of them faced. (Why are bonfires built prior to November 5th a great danger to hedgehogs?) The children thought of words that might be used to describe an ideal home for a hedgehog — safe, cosy, soft, warm, leaves, round, strong, waterproof, away from badgers. In groups the children then planned and built the sort of homes that they felt the hedgehogs might like (see photographs). Model hedgehogs made from potatoes and matchsticks took up residence in the homes.

CHRISTCHURCH SCHOOL, ST LEONARDS

Young children will enjoy giving their creatures an identity and telling of their adventures just as five year old Catherine has done below:

Prickley and Spikey went out one night to look for food and they found slugs and snails and made piggies of themselve

An excellent link with such activity would be *The Hodgeheg* by Dick King-Smith (Young Puffin 1989). The story looks at the problems faced by hedgehogs when they try to cross roads. In this instance a busy road lies between the hedgehog family in number 5A and the park which they all dream of reaching. Young Max (or to give him his full title — Victor Maximillian St. George) is determined to find out how humans manage to cross safely and his adventures will promote much discussion as to how we might avoid the nightly carnage of small creatures crossing our roads.

The children at Christchurch School had also considered why animals such as badgers and rabbits are killed. 'Hunter's think that it's fun,' one lad commented. This might be a suitable point to read Roald Dahl's *The Magic Finger* (Young Puffin 1974). This is a short story that revolves around a young girl who is able to put the magic finger on people when she sees something really wicked and cruel happening. One thing that really makes her mad is when she sees people shooting animals for fun and one day she puts the magic finger on her neighbours when they come home from shooting ducks. Many children will feel that the family get what they deserve and there should be some interesting discussion concerning the story's outcome. Follow it up by considering how other creatures might get their own back on man's cruelty. Perhaps some children might enjoy writing down such a story and illustrating it.

In the Countryside written by Jakki Wood and published by Hodder & Stoughton in their *Naturewalks* series (1989) takes the children on a walk into the country by means of a story that develops on the left hand side of each page, with information about the plants and creatures that they encounter on the right hand side.

JAKKI WOODS, NATURE WALKS IN THE COUNTRYSIDE, 1989 (HODDER AND STOUGHTON)

If it is possible to take the children on a walk into the country it will be fun to write in a similar way. In groups the children could record what they see at each stage of their walk — Karen saw a ladybird, Ellen found blackberries, Robert caught his foot in a rabbit hole, Lisa found fungi. The information page about fungi might then include a warning about the dangers of mistaking toadstools for mushrooms. The same walk can be undertaken at different times of the year and the observations recorded and compared.

Some children may well be inspired to look at one particular discovery in more detail:

The Blackberry

A glossy clump of purple blobs
Green ones at the top like knots
Purple ones have a soft flesh
Sweetening day by day
Pick it and it snaps
So juicy in your mouth

So sweet
I want more and more

EMILY BYHAM (AGE 7)

Can the children think of reasons why hedgerows are important in the countryside? They offer shelter for plants to grow and thrive, and for animals to breed. There are many food chains in a hedgerow. (Some work on simple food chains may be appropriate here.) They also offer shelter to farm animals from the wind, rain and snow. However, hedgerows are disappearing at a fast rate as farmers enlarge their fields to suit bigger machinery. Children might find it interesting to conduct a month-by-month survey of a nearby hedge to discover the sort of creatures and plants that enjoy its protection. Simple note-taking and tabulation could be encouraged here:

Position of hedge ....

Date ....

Time ....

Plants noted ....

Creatures spotted ....

The progress of particular plants could be measured and commented on, along with appropriate sketches and/or photographs. If possible, obtain a copy of *In the Hedgerow* by Nathalie Tordjman (Moonlight Publishing 1990) which contains much information about hedges, their origins and functions, plus a month-by-month review of the animal and plant life that children might expect to find.

Although most people would agree about protecting animal and plant life, there are some animals that cause great problems to farmers. There are many insects that can destroy large areas of crops, birds often steal seeds, and a fox can cause havoc with ducks and chickens. Talk to the children about the problems that farmers face. How do they control pests? What are the dangers of widespread use of pesticides? Mention the effects on food chains and how pesticides can be washed off fields into streams. If possible, ask a local farmer into the classroom to talk to the children about his work. They may have some searching questions to put to him!

Alternatively, pay a visit to a farm. City schools may well find that there are city farms close by. Such a visit can be a sensory experience — plenty to smell, touch, see and hear. Children could be asked to record their findings in lists that may well be developed further in the classroom.

On the Farm

Smelling
The foul stench in the pig sty
The freshness of the grain
The creamy smell in the milking parlour
The newly ploughed fields
The bulls eating their food
The lambs jumping in the field

Feeling
The dry dusty grain in the sheds
The smooth warm eggs
The rough curly fur of the kids

Hearing
The bleating of the sheep
And the chickens clucking
And the squealing of the piglets

Thinking
About what the farmer is saying
About all I have seen
And wondering if I will come again.

JAMES HALL

Children may also enjoy producing farming calendars — month-by-month on the farm. Again much information could be obtained from a visit to a farm or from inviting a farmer to talk to the class. Prior to the visit, ask the children to come up with their own ideas as to what might happen each month on a farm. Discuss in groups and pool results. Talk about city farms — an attempt to bring something of the countryside into an urban environment. What problems might they face? How would they differ from country farms? A frieze might be produced to show the farm surrounded by warehouses and blocks of flats. Children might have fun sequencing the following poem and producing captioned illustrations in the form of a storyboard:

The City Farm

There were goats and ducks and chickens
to see at the city farm.
'Watch out for the goose — he goes for your knees',
we turned around in alarm.
But the goose must have been really tired
and although he opened one eye
to gaze long and hard at both of us,
he decided to let us slip by.
We watched the cows being milked
and a goat took food from my hands,
we spread seed around for the chickens
and bottle fed baby lambs.
We stared at a huge mother sow

with ten piglets all running about,
then tried to sneak back past the goose
but he honked and chased us both out!

BRIAN MOSES

Ask if children know about the country code. Explain that it is a list of rules which advise people how to behave correctly in the countryside. Children in groups could discuss what these rules might be and make up their own. Lists can be compared with each other and then with the country code itself. In pairs, children could take one of the rules and produce as a poster which will inform others of the need to take care. Short stories could be written based on each of the twelve rules, showing how negligence caused unnecessary suffering or damage. These could then be acted out and presented to other classes. Such a presentation might well include a performance of the following piece where the poet John Foster has incorporated the country code into his poem:

We must protect the countryside

We must protect the countryside —
The flowers and the trees.
We must protect the animals.
It's up to you and me.

Don't throw litter on the ground.
Please put it in a bin,
And close the gate behind you
To keep the cattle in.

Keep your dog upon a lead.
Make sure it doesn't stray.
Stay on the paths. Don't wander
Through fields of wheat or hay.

Don't leave a broken bottle
Lying on the grass
Or it could start a fire
Like a magnifying glass.

Don't poke around in birds' nests
Or chase creatures that you see.
Don't pull up plants or flowers
Or break branches off a tree.

Don't squeeze through gaps in hedges.
Please use the stiles or gates.
Don't pollute the water
With rubbish or lead weights.

We must protect the animals,
the trees, the plants, the flowers.
We must protect the countryside.
Remember that it's ours.

JOHN FOSTER

Reading Resources

Poetry

A First Poetry Book (OUP 1979) includes Eleanor Farjeon's 'A Dragonfly' and John Kitching's 'Slugs'. *Another First Poetry Book* (OUP 1987) includes 'In the Wood' by Sheila Simmons, 'Feather or Fur' by John Becker, 'Crows' by David McCord plus poems about the seasons. Both books compiled by John Foster.

Fox Poems and *Seed Poems,* both compiled by John Foster (Jackdaws, OUP 1990).

I Like That Stuff: Poems from many Cultures selected by Morag Styles (CUP 1984). Section on 'Birds, beasts and butterflies'.

Poems for 7 Year Olds and Under chosen by Helen Nicoll (Kestrel 1983/Puffin 1984). Two useful sections 'Fur and Feather' and 'Leaping and Creeping'.

The Squirrel in Town and other nature poems by Stanley Cook (Blackie 1988). A lovely collection and a marvellous resource for 'Where can I find a poem about . . .?' questions.

Fiction

Attila The Hen by Paddy Mounter (Yearling 1991). Attila is a big, stroppy hen who has no intention of being cooped up in a dirty, smelly battery farm. She plans a daring escape — for herself and all her sisters.

Meet the Greens by Sue Limb (Orchard Books 1988). Lizzie Green 'kidnaps' one of Mr Dewey's hens in her fight with him over factory-farming.

The World that Jack Built, written and illustrated by Ruth Brown (Anderson Press 1990). Based on the rhyme 'The House that Jack Built' this picture book features a black cat exploring two valleys, one unspoilt and the other polluted by a factory built by Jack. Splendid pictures and a powerful message.

Who Am I? by Richard Watson (Picture Corgi 1991). A small prickly animal wakes up one spring day to find that he has no memory of who he is. Lovely picture book for very young children.

Non-fiction

Countryside Handbook by Michael Chinnery (Kingfisher 1990). More suitable for seven and eight year olds. A survey of the various habitats for wild creatures and plants throughout Britain.

Farming Now; Conservation by Joy Palmer (Hodder ahd Stoughton 1989). Why is conservation important and how does it affect us?

Starting Points: Spring, Summer, Autumn, Winter by Ruth Thomson — four volumes (Franklin Watts 1989). Packed with information about the various seasons and ideas for crafts and other activities.

The Kingfisher Book of 1001 Questions and Answers: Animals by Michele Staple and Linda Gamlin (Kingfisher Books 1990). A really handy reference book for those awkward questions such as 'Do frogs climb trees?' and 'How do ants communicate?'

The Roadside (Bellamy's Changing World) by David Bellamy, illustrated by Jill Dow (Macdonald). A look at animal and plant life patterns along the roadside. A wealth of illustrative material — plenty to talk about. Other titles in the same series — *The Forest, The Rockpool, The River*.

The Usborne Complete First Book of Nature (Usborne 1990). Usual high standard of presentation and illustrative detail. A fascinating compendium for the classroom.

Worm's Eye View: Make your own wildlife park and be friends with small animals by Kipchak Johnson (Cassell 1990). Original presentation showing children how to make a wildlife park in their back gardens, how to handle small animals, making a pond, and why worms are so important.

24 Hours in a Forest by Barrie Watts (Franklin Watts 1990). Outstanding photography, many close-up shots covering the animals, insects and plants to be found in a forest throughout the day and night.

Parks and Playgrounds

 A visit to a nearby park may help children to appreciate what a park has to offer and lead them to speculate on what other features might be desirable.

Prior to a visit spend some time exploring what the children already know about parks. List everything that they have discovered in the parks that they have visited. Children in groups could talk about how parks change their appearance according to the time of year. Ask what happens to the shapes of trees as the seasons pass. Do the children know why trees lose their leaves in Autumn or why bulbs begin to grow in Winter?

Encourage children to think in advance about the problems of looking after parks. Discuss what these might be and then prior to setting out, decide on something that the children will focus on — how tidy is the park, are there enough litter bins, what about safety precautions around ponds and play areas?

Equip some children with a cassette recorder so that they are able to speak about what they find. They could also read out from notices in the park so that these can be considered back in the classroom. Someone at work in the park may be prepared to answer a few questions or perhaps an appointment can be made with the park keeper and questions prepared previously.

Items of interest can be collected for close examination back at school. Small children can work in pairs or in groups to talk about what they have discovered, to make detailed drawings and to write about their experiences:

Conkers

Like lots of small
Light green hedgehogs,
With sharp spikes
On their backs,
Lying on the grass.
Inside are chocolate brown conkers,
Smooth, round and cold.

ROLAND NICHOLLS (AGE 8) CADBURY'S 4th CHILDREN'S POETRY (BEAVER)

Dry leaves crunch,
Dry leaves crackle,
Dry leaves feel crispy.

(AGE 5)

Trish Vaughan and her class of seven year olds at Hollington Junior School in Hastings visited Alexandra Park. Previously the children had been asked to count the number of litter bins as a start to observational work. However they discovered lots of things that they thought were wrong — weeds, graffiti, litter, safety measures around the ponds, and swamp-like areas which were difficult to see. The children were asked to use all their senses and to remember things that they saw, heard, touched, smelled and tasted.

(In the above list is a complaint about weeds. How do children react to the view that weeds are really just wild plants which *we* consider to be growing in the wrong place? Consider too, how parks could encourage the development of 'wild areas' where plants and small creatures may thrive unhindered. Do the children know of any such areas locally?)

Back at school it was decided that letters should be written to inform people about the park.

Here, of course, is an opportunity to discuss letter writing in general. What form will the letters take? How will they be written? What 'voice' will be chosen? Talk about how you wouldn't expect to write the same sort of letter to the park keeper or the editor of a local paper as you would to a relation. Letters should be courteous, carefully thought out and neatly written. In this instance, mention should be made of what was good about the park as well as what was considered wrong. One group's letter to the local paper is printed below:

Dear Editor,
On Monday 25th June we went to Alexandra Park. We enjoyed it but the toilets are foul. It was nice looking at the ducks but there were no railings. The swings were from 2 - 4 year olds. The flower beds were lovely. We liked feeding the ducks but we were disgusted about the pond because there was rubbish in the pond.

Please print our letter as we think it can be improved.

Yours faithfully,

DAVID TEMPLE (AGE 8), COLIN MATTHEWS (AGE 7), TIMOTHY HARRIS (AGE 8), MATTHEW HESMAN (AGE 8) AND BEN ADAMS (AGE 8).

Later a further group were interviewed for a report in another paper:

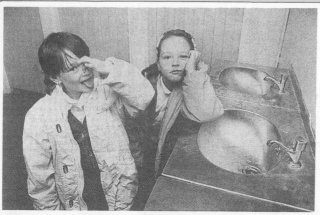

Pooh! Class 4 turn up their noses at park

● Gemma Richardson and Suzanne Kelly are sniffy about the state of the ladies' toilets (left). Colin Matthews and Martyn Rogers (right) help keep the park clean.

by ALISON FLOOD

SMELLY loos, dog mess, litter and graffiti prompted Class 4 of Hollington Junior School to fire off complaining letters to the council last week.

The class spent a day at Alexandra Park with teacher Trish Vaughan, but they turned their noses up at what they found.

One letter said: "We were disgusted about the girls' toilets. They were very smelly."

Hayley Deeprose, 8, said: "There was a lot of dog mess, too. We only saw one person clear it up and a couple of people pick up litter. The dogs weren't kept on leads, and some were quite big."

The class think there whould be more litter bins — they only saw about a dozen while walking the whole length of the park — and suggest there should be a park warden.

They are also worried about the lack of warning signs around ponds and streams.

"If you were not looking you could have just walked into the ponds because there was no fencing. Where there was fencing it was not high enough. There was a sign for the little railway, but it was in the pond. By the time we had worked out what it said we had already walked all over the track," said Martyn Rogers, eight.

There are lots of things the children do like, though.

Suzanne, Gemma, Clare, Sara, Chanel and Esther said: "We thought the flower beds were nice and it was very nice to have a shop in the park. The ducks were very nice, the trees were lovely and we like the squirrels."

Carly, Martyn, Christopher, Shelley and Nicola particularly enjoyed feeding the ducks, and looking at the birds and flowers.

Suzanne Kelly said afterwards: "We had a great time and saw lots of lovely things. I'd like to go back."

Mrs Vaughan said: "We have been doing lots of work on conservation and the environment recently and the children are very aware. It's good that they notice these things."

Council parks chief Bob Dawson said there is no park warden because the council cannot afford one.

"I'm very sorry the girls thought the toilets were smelly, but I'm having trouble getting an attendant. We've had two already this year, but they've left. It's not a very pleasant job."

Mr Dawson thinks there are enough litter bins, but added: "We cannot help that people do not put their litter or dog mess into the bins provided."

HASTINGS AND ST LEONARDS OBSERVER, JULY 12, 1990

Following on from such a visit, much talk will be speculative — How might the litter problem in a park be solved? What can be done to combat vandalism? How can play areas be improved? Are safety precautions adequate?

Several children from Hollington School wrote to the Director of Tourism and Leisure to seek his views:

'We keep providing litter bins but only this morning, the Supervisor in charge of the Park has advised me that one was damaged over the weekend and will have to be replaced, also 6 seats were sprayed with paint and will have to be taken into the workshop and cleaned. I would like to provide more litter bins, but I have a limit on the amount of money that I can spend and unfortunately a lot of this is spent on replacing bins damaged and broken by vandals.'

The letter writers were happy with their reply, deciding that teenagers were to blame and that they wouldn't be like *that!* It was decided that posters might be an effective way of discouraging vandalism, and that the posters should be in bright, fluorescent colours, aimed at a teenage audience.

A discussion of how the actions of others affect what we are able to do might be relevant here. Seven year olds at St Leonards C.E. School were very concerned about the state of nearby parks and play areas —'Too many people dropping litter, swings broken or twisted round their frames, plants broken or pulled up, dogs fouling play areas . . .'. A similar catalogue of complaints could probably be drawn up anywhere. In their opinion, signs and notices didn't deter. Even adults still allowed their dogs to foul playgrounds despite signs that warned of penalties.

From such actions that are detrimental to others at a local level, consider what happens at a national or international level. What are the problems that affect others globally? Can what happens in one country affect the livelihood of another? Think about the rubbish that's dropped in a river and is then carried by the river's flow into neighbouring countries.

Further speculative talk could focus on the changing park. How would the park look at night? Again go through the senses. There would be much more to hear — rustling in the undergrowth, distant sounds of passing cars, perhaps the cries of small creatures. Compare day and night in the park, draw pictures to show differences.

DANIELLE DULCE (AGE 6)

Ian Souter's poem is about visiting a park on a Sunday in Autumn:

Early Last Sunday Morning

Early last Sunday morning,
Dad said we needed a glass of fresh air
and a mouthful of greeness.
So off we slipped to the nearby park
where we crept in as soundless as snails.
Around us the day breathed air
that was as sharp as vinegar,
Reminding us that winter was on its way.

Inside we watched the trees stretch and wake
while the grass stood up and shivered.
Soon I was pointing towards a spider
that was strung on a necklace web.

While behind it,
The sun rolled out like a golden ball.

Dad smiled,
as a squirrel scampered from a bush
then turned to grey stone,
until with a flick of its tail
it waved goodbye and was gone.

Later as we passed the children's playground,
I looked at the lonely red slide
and briefly remembered the summer days
when I flew its long slippery tongue.
But a cold wind pushed me past
until I just let the warmth in my dad's hand
lead me on home.

Read the above poem (without its title) and ask the children to think which season of the year is being described. Emphasise that they should offer you a reasoned response and not a guess. Then read the poem a second time and ask for a favourite line or idea. What attracts them to their particular choices?

Let the children draw a response to the poem — the glass of fresh air, the necklace web, the sun rolling out like a golden ball, the slide and its long slippery tongue.

Discuss what could be seen at other times in the park — on a sunny Sunday afternoon, a winter dusk, a snowy day, in drizzle or a high wind. Write down the ideas. Can the ideas be rearranged into a poem?

Alternatively write about how the park changes with the seasons. Read *The Tree in Season* by Robert Fisher from *Another Second Poetry Book* ed. John Foster (O.U.P.).

A list could be made of the kind of plants that children might expect to find growing in our parks. Suggest that they search out pictures of unusual plants that thrive because conditions are particularly favourable e.g. palm trees on the South Devon coast, banana trees in the Botanical Pleasure gardens at Ventnor on the Isle of Wight, exotic varieties at Kew Gardens or the Botanic Gardens in Cambridge. Where do these plants normally grow?

Try to find pictures of species of plants that grow in other parts of the world but not in Britain. How does the weather affect the kinds of plant life that grows naturally in countries where the climate is different to ours? Why does a cactus grow to a gigantic size in the Arizona desert? Why can't we grow cactus plants in our parks and gardens? What special conditions do they need?

Hollington children were critical of the play facilities in their local park, judging them only suitable for pre-school children. In this instance, children might be asked to talk about what they would like to see provided in the park. Later, plans might be drawn up to show where equipment could be sited. Lists of rules could be devised for the safe use of the play area. What should be done with anyone who deliberately damaged the area?

Suggest that children design their ideal play area. Give them some idea of the size of area that they will be considering e.g. an area the size of the school playground or the school hall so that they can begin to think in terms of what will fit into the available space. Often it is best to work in pairs so that suggestions can be considered and discussed. List the items that might be included — slides, swings, see-saw, scramble net, climbing frame, roundabout, sand pit etc. Check that there are facilities for all kinds of physical activity —

jumping, climbing, swinging, balancing etc. Then think about where the equipment will be placed. What sort of surface should the playground have? Do the children know about the special type of surface that is used for children's playgrounds today? What was wrong with concrete or tarmac as surface material? How will the playground be made to look attractive? Will there be trees, flower beds, hanging baskets, benches? What about items for very small children?

Some children might then go on to model their playgrounds. One pair could be linked with another, and advice sought as to how their playgrounds might be improved. Much discussion could take place on the choice of appropriate modelling materials and the best ways of using them — how do you get a swing to swing?

TIMMY WISE AND STEPHEN WILSON

Reading Resources

Child Education: March 1988 — *Parks*.

In the Park by Jakki Wood (Naturewalks series — Hodder & Stoughton 1989). This book is a lively mix of fiction and non-fiction where a visit to the park is accompanied by information about the various creatures, plants and trees that are seen there.

Look Around the Park by Clive Pace and Jean Birch (Wayland 1989). All sorts of park activities — playgrounds, food, special events, the unusual, along with animals, birds, flowers and trees. Simple but informative text and good photography.

My Class visit a Park by Vicki Lee (Franklin Watts 1985). A photographic record of a class trip to a London park with one pupil relating her thoughts on what they see there.

Nothing to be Afraid Of — Jan Mark (Viking/Puffin). Short Stories. The first of these is a real winner. Anthea shows little nervous Robin around the park visiting 'Leopard Walk' and 'Poison Alley', and meeting up with the 'Greasy Witch' and the 'Lavatory Demon'. Seven and eight year olds will love it!

Park: Through the Seasons by Deni Brown (Wayland 1989). A look at the changing park over the course of a year. Lots of ideas for things to do and to look out for when visiting a park.

The Seashore

TALK about the seashore — who has visited the sea, where did they go, what did they do there? On a map of Great Britain mark in the places that children have visited. Perhaps there is a holiday postcard or picture of the resort that could be pinned alongside it. Has anyone visited a beach in another country?

Play *I Packed my Bag . . .* around the class as you make up a list of items that you would need to take with you on a trip to the sea — towel, bucket and spade, flask, sandwiches, fruit, sun tan oil, sunglasses, shrimping net, arm bands etc. What sort of list would you make for a winter visit to the seashore?

Read John Prater's *The Perfect Day* (Bodley Head 1986/Picture Corgi 1989). In this account of a visit to the seaside, everyone is having a wonderful time except Kevin. However, at the end of the book something special happens and Kevin begins to enjoy himself after all. Discuss what things the children enjoy, or don't enjoy about the seaside. Make lists of good and bad points. Would everyone's lists be the same?

A visit to the seaside might well be an opportunity for drama. Children in groups could prepare a short scene including being stuck in a traffic jam, beach activities, a picnic on the sand, a lost child, sheltering from the rain, the journey home etc. Alternatively John Prater's *The Perfect Day* could be acted out.

Set up space for a display area and encourage children to bring to school any seaside related items — souvenirs, gifts, postcards, shells etc. Can anyone bring in a jar of coloured sands, a stick of seaside rock, a shrimping net, bucket and spade, old photographs of the seaside, holiday brochures etc? Write notices yourself or help children to write about where the items came from. Encourage the children to choose an item, look at it closely and then sketch it. Include these drawings in the display.

A visit to the seashore is a bonus for any sea project. Collect interesting items from the beach — shells, shaped stones, sea-bleached wood, and so on. These can be labelled, drawn and perhaps written about back at school. Prior to writing, share discoveries and brainstorm for words and phrases that best describe the items. A smooth colourful pebble might well have magic properties: 'With my magic stone I can call up a genie who will give me three wishes.' 'With my magic stone I can . . .'.

Talk about life on the seashore and how care needs to be taken in searching out small creatures. Remind the children that when investigating beneath a rock they must be careful to replace the rock and avoid damaging crabs and other small creatures in the process. Should children take home creatures that are found on the shore? What would happen to them without the right conditions? Perhaps a set of rules can be suggested and written out relating to conduct on the seashore.

Some children will enjoy making their own picture books that give information about the seashore. These can be done in a number of ways although a book that is written for a specified audience will give the writer a sense of purpose. Books can be written for friends to read or for younger children.Lift the flap books are fun and children will be familiar with examples of the genre — Eric Hill's *'Spot'* books, Rod Campbell's *'Dear Zoo'* etc.

Books that the children produce can pose questions. Answers can then be revealed when a child lifts a flap which is part of a drawing. Who lives in this rock pool? A crab. What's that lying on the sand? A starfish. What can you see fixed to the rock? A limpet.

Other children may prefer to list clues that help us to identify the creature in hiding. This creature:

> lives in a rock pool
> has a shell and six legs
> can nip your fingers . . .
>
> Answer ....
>
> *Now lift the flap to see if you were right.*

Other children may prefer to gather information about sea creatures and then to present their findings for a wall display. Perhaps they can also tell the rest of the class about their work. Some lines of research will lead them to form opinions about the way in which particular forms of sea life are treated.

> ### The Seal
>
> I think the Seal looks so beautiful and I love Them for one reason: the pus are fuffy and They make me laugh But What is sad is The men killing the Poor Seals. Some ladies don't care They would Father have a Fuffy coat.
>
> LUCY NOVIS

Shells can be classified in a number of ways — type, size, colour, shape — and some interesting imagery can result from discussions about their appearance. Read Robin Mellor's poem and listen out for his ideas:

Collecting Shells

I like to look for shells on the beach.
Mum gets some bags for us, one each
and we go to see what we can find;
it isn't long before I fill mine.

I've got cowrie shells, white and brown,
a flat round shell shaped like a crown,
an oyster shell with Mother of Pearl,
a water snail, wound up in a curl.

Pink and yellow, brown and white,
one like the sun, or the moon at night.
I found a dead crab inside one shell,
but left it there because of the smell.

I keep the shells on my bedroom shelf
like jewels I have collected myself.
All year they're there, within my reach,
to remind me of my day at the beach.

ROBIN MELLOR

If there are any large shells, suggest that the children put them to their ears and listen to the sounds of the sea. What sort of message is it sending?

The Song of the Sea

I hear sand being washed into the sea.
Fishes breathing in rock pools.
The swish of a catfish's tail.
The clamp of limpets moving on rocks
Sea anemones, tentacles grabbing
The chorus of porpoise singing
Water scorpions scampering under seaweed and
Rocks to hide
Crabs cracking their nippers
Sea-gulls chorusing above the waves
Shells washed upon the beach
Seaweed floating on the tide
Underwater echoes of colonies of barnacles
Gossiping
Shrimps breathing underwater
Shell fishes creeping into their shells
Octopuses sliding on rocks
Water worms digging

Dolphins leaping and diving
Whales spurting salt water up skyward
Stones and pebbles splatting the shining ultra-marine Sea.
Bivalves opening gradually in the deep dark sea.

NEIL RICHARDS (AGE 8)

Any prose or poetry that arises from observation and discussion can be mounted alongside drawings and displayed in class folders or zig-zag books.

Perhaps the sand tray or another area might be turned into a model beach with a wall frieze behind it. What sort of beach will it be — a holiday resort with a background of hotels, arcades and a funfair, or somewhere less accessible with dunes, a rocky shore and wildlife? Allow children to suggest ideas, to put alternative viewpoints and then to vote as to what they would like included in the model. Is the beach safe for bathing? If not, will there be warning notices? What sort of people might visit their beach and for what reasons? What would be the good and bad points about the beach? Could it be improved in any way?

Younger children can produce alphabet books of their seaside visit which will again draw their attention back to what they saw and heard. A good example of this approach is *By the Sea: An Alphabet Book* by Ann Blades (CUP 1987) — Xx shows two children x-ing with a stick on damp sand!

On most trips to the seashore these days there is usually a fair sprinkle of litter along the tideline. Some of this will have been left by beach visitors, and some will have been washed ashore. An alternative alphabet of beach finds might survey such items. These could be collected in sacks after first warning children about taking care when handling objects. (Warn in advance and encourage children to bring along old gloves.)

On one particular beach survey that I took part in, a variety of cans were discovered. There were some that hadn't been on the beach for long while others were rusted and unidentifiable. A couple were battered and split, while another had been 'peeled' open like apple skin. The children's favourite was a can that had been flattened vertically and reduced to a height of 5 cms!

After the rubbish collection, arrange the children in a circle with everyone sitting on the sand. Pass round the bag and ask each child to reach in and pull out a piece of litter. (Again, children should wear gloves for this.) Then give them a minute or two to think up a story to explain how their item came to be on the shore. Later these could be written down:

The plastic cup is broken and torn. I think a family were having a picnic and drinking lemonade. A wasp fell in the lemonade and the little girl threw it away.

The can is rusty. It is bent. I think that some big children threw stones at it.

The lolly wrapper was thrown away by a little girl. She bought the lolly from the ice cream van.

Once plausible reasons have been found for the litter being on the beach, tell stories that give fantastic reasons — the crushed can was sat on by a giant, a piece of wood was burnt by dragon's breath, a small plastic spoon belonged to a mermaid, and so on.

Suggest that the children draw pictures to illustrate their ideas. Mount them side by side along with written explanations; one possible, one fantastic.

Try to discover where some of the rubbish comes from. Much of it will be home-produced but there may be items from abroad that have found their way to our shore.

Classify the rubbish into items that will rot and items that won't. Aluminium cans and bottles can be taken from the beach for recycling.

How do the children feel about the litter that they find on beaches? List the dangers that litter causes — broken glass and sharp edged tins are hazards to beach users, old fishing line and nets are hazards for seabirds. Plastic bags kill sea creatures — turtles often mistake plastic bags for jellyfish and the bags become lodged in their throats.

Design a poster to warn people how dangerous it can be to leave litter on the beaches. How will the poster be worded? Keep it simple for maximum impact.

Make sure children understand that all life forms on the seashore are closely dependent on each other. The seashore supplies food for many breds of birds. The twice daily tidal changeround brings plankton (microscopic animals and plants) to many creatures that hide away in rock pools. If the sea is dirty or fouled with oil or chemicals, the plankton cannot survive and the food chain collapses. Make up examples of food chains such as:

SEAL — FISH — PLANKTON ANIMALS — PLANKTON PLANTS.

The different members of the chain can be drawn, cut out and hung up as mobiles.

Check the beach for signs of oil. (It will often be picked up on shoes!) Why is there oil on the beaches? What are the problems that it causes? Has anyone heard of oil being spilt into the sea recently? Have there been any pictures on the television?

Suggest that children work in groups and prepare their own news item about oil being spilt into the sea. Mention where it came from, how it happened, who is to blame and what can be done. Some children might care to 'broadcast' their news item to the class or at a school assembly.

Read Matt Simpson's poem 'Oil Spill'. Why does he compare the oil to treacle? Do oil and treacle feel the same? What words might be used to describe them both?

What creature is Matt Simpson thinking about when he writes about the oil's *filthy tentacles*?

Oil Spill

huge slow stain
smudging the tide

crude black slime
fouling the river

filthy tentacles
groping the banks

a deadly treacle
a vile slobber
an evil sludge

suffocating everything.

MATT SIMPSON

Reading Resources

Poetry

A Very First Poetry Book, A First Poetry Book, Another First Poetry Book — all edited by John Foster (O.U.P.). These are worth looking through for appropriate sea poems.

Poems for Seven Year Olds and Under chosen by Helen Nicholl (Young Puffin 1984). This has a section on the *Sea and Shore* including several well-known poems.

Poems to Paddle in compiled by Raymond Wilson (Hutchinson 1989). A strong and varied collection. Includes Kit Wrights's 'Let's hear it for the limpet'.

Sea Poems compiled by John Foster (Jackdaws Poetry: Oxford Reading Tree 1990). A slim volume of seaside poems for young children. Poems about lighthouses, sandcastles, pebbles, shells and gulls.

Fiction

At the Beach by Anne and Harlow Rockwell (Hamish Hamilton 1988). Simple story of things to do on the beach, climbing sand dunes, collecting shells and having a picnic.

Lucy and Tom at the Seaside by Shirley Hughes (Picture Corgi). Joys of the seaside explored plus some lovely pictures.

Max and Diana and the Beach Day by Harriet Ziefert (Viking Kestrel 1987). Twins spend a day at the beach finding shells, building castles etc.

The Lighthouse Keeper's Rescue by Ronda and David Armitage (Andre Deutsch 1989). A further tale of Mr. Grinling's exploits. This time he's about to be sacked from his duties through falling asleep but his involvement in the rescue of a beached whale earns him a reprieve.

The Water Horse by Dick King-Smith (Viking 1990). Kirstie and Angus discover a washed-up 'egg' on the beach. Baby Crusoe hatches out and soon outgrows his fishpond. Where now for the water-horse? Dick King-Smith has written an engaging story that considers an unusual aspect of conservation and offers a possible 'answer' to one of the world's great mysteries!

Non-fiction

Around the Coast by Mark C. W. Sleep (Wayland, Young Explorer Books 1983). More suited to seven and eight year olds. Clear explanations of waves, tides and currents, beach and cave formation. Touches on pollution.

What Can I See? At the Seaside by Cecilia Fitzsimons (Hamish Hamilton 1990). Good introduction to the animals and plants that live on the seashore.

24 Hours On a Seashore by Barrie Watts (Frankling Watts 1990). Superb photographs and informative text depicting a day in the life of a stretch of shoreline and how plants and creatures adapt their behaviour to changes in tides and temperature.

Teachers' Book

Ocean Challenge by Bob Foster-Smith (WWF UK 1990). This is an ideas pack for teachers of children between the ages of 7 and 13 — 'An Educational Journey Across the Oceans'. The pack is cross-curricular and provides teachers with opportunities to introduce environmental considerations — and marine issues in particular — into their everyday classroom teaching. All the material is designed around a voyage — designing a boat, finding the way, dealing with the elements etc. Ideas could easily be adapted for younger children.

Water

Water

Water's found — as nature rules —
in many shapes: ponds, rivers, pools,

streams, lakes, drops, trickles, splashes, showers,
canned, bottled, in the stems of flowers,

not to mention leaves, roots, petals,
also trees, and often kettles,

tea pots, tea cups, fizzy drinks,
toilets, baths, bowls, buckets, sinks,

gurgling full of leaves down drains,
pouring in torrential rains,

pumped out by the heart in blood,
churned in earth to squelchy mud,

used by dad to wash his car,
mixed in jam inside a jar,

pounding round a washing machine,
keeping lawns a decent green,

squirting out of water pistols,
forming snow from tiny crystals,

making medicines and lotions,
filling earth with massive oceans.

There's something magical about it.
Where would we all be without it?

CHARLES THOMSON

READ Charles Thomson's poem a couple of times and then ask the children to try and remember all the different places where water is found and the uses to which it is put. Turn this into a test of memory akin to the 'objects on a tray' game. Older children can work in groups, talking about their lists while younger ones work collectively as a class.

Next check to see whether the poet has missed out any important items. Sub-divide lists into water in the home, in the garden, in the community etc. List the ways in which we use water during the course of a day. Some children may like to produce a 'storyboard' with illustrations alongside each item.

Talk about wasting water. How is it possible to waste water? What can be done to prevent water from being wasted in the areas mentioned above? Some children may care to produce posters encouraging others to conserve water. Talk about what should be depicted on such posters, think of slogans. Design badges.

What does water look like? Does it change its appearance at different locations? What colour is it? How does it feel? Children could make a list of their observations:

Colourful like the sky,
greeny-blue like eyes,
see-through like tears,
silky like a nightie,
glitters like gold,
cool like the feel when you jump in a pool,
wavy like the jacuzzi

ALISON YOUNGSON (AGE 8)

Where does water come from? A brief explanation of the water cycle may be appropriate followed by first-hand observation of water on a rainy day. Observe the action of water, on the school playground and field, in the drains, pipes and gutters. Try to observe small rivulets transporting dust, sand, leaves, twigs and other material.

Younger children can make observations about the rain, why they like or dislike it, while older children can begin to think of water as a changing force in the landscape.

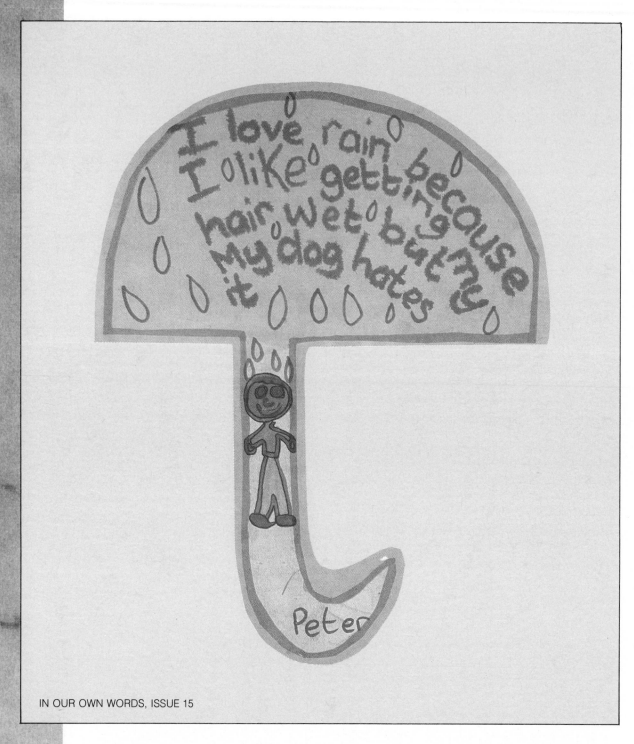

IN OUR OWN WORDS, ISSUE 15

For children who are learning to read, *By the Stream* written by Roderick Hunt for the Oxford Reading Tree is a humorous accompaniment to any stream visit. Sticks are dropped into the water, followed by a teddy bear which everyone attempts to rescue.

Prior to any stream or river visit, prepare a list of questions that will assist children in writing a river report on their return to school. Discuss with the children, or allow them to talk in groups about the kinds of questions that will lead to useful information being gathered. What is the river/stream called? Where did you visit it? How wide is it? What did you see/hear/smell? What wildlife did you see? Could any rubbish be seen in the river or on the banks and if so, where do you think it came from? Are there any signs of pollution — foam or soap suds, a shiny film on the surface, an awful smell?

If possible, try to visit rivers or streams in two contrasting areas — country and city. Talk about the differences.

Where does the river begin? Where does it reach the sea? Check that children understand which way a river flows. Observe the flow on visits. With the aid of pictures, talk about what happens to a river on its journey to the sea, how it begins in the hills, becomes a small stream and then widens. Think about the different sorts of landscape that it passes through, the buildings that might be seen on its banks, the bridges that cross it and the wildlife that is visible in different parts.

Some children might like to tell the story of a river. Children can work in groups and decide what happens to their river on its journey from source to sea. With younger children, a wall frieze can depict the different sections with children adding words and illustrations.

The two pieces of writing included below may assist children in thinking about how they might tell the story of a river:

The River

I gurgle
Twisting and turning
I go
Babbling,
Tinkling,
Dripping over rocks
For I am a little river.
Now I am bigger
Fish swim in me
High above I see
Wellington boots.
Man builds houses beside me
I am powerful
Suspension bridges hang above me
But I am spoiled
Muddy am I
There I end in the sea
But I do not die
For high above
I am still young.

SUSANNA TAYLER (AGE 6)

IN OUR OWN WORDS, ISSUE 15

The Little Trickle

It had been a very hard winter and a lot of snow had fallen.
The snow had started to melt and sevral little trickles started
to run down the mountain. Soon other trickles joined up with
it and maid a stream which hurried down the mountain. Soon
it was about 2 metres wide and you could call it a tiny river.
The river was now in the wild country and was flowing fairly
fast. Some minnows were swimming in the river. It was now 6

metres wide, swirling fast and was coming into the farm country. (It had 295 miles to go before the sea.)

Every 2 miles was a farm and you could see a church spire. The river went under a bridge and on the other side were some children sailing boats. Further along the bank some Otters came out and splashed about. The river went through a village and came out the other side it went through the country for a time and then came to another village after that it was just soil it went on for about 3 days. Then one night the river froze over and stopped the water supply for a week. It was now about 14 metres wide and had 45 miles to go before the estuary. So it decided to hurry all the more (very) excited and happy. It was now coming to the outskirts of Stratford upon Avon. It was getting deeper, wider and nearer every minute and was also getting faster it had just gone past the Shakespeare theatre and was going quite fast when it came to a lock. It wanted to keep going. It couldn't wait there was no time to hang around. It seemed to say 'keep going keep going keep going I mustn't lose time keep going keep going keep going' or 'I'm late I'm late I mustn't wait I'm late I'm late I'm late'. But soon it was hurrying along especially fast to make up for lost time. When people went by it they would say 'look at that river hurrying by what's the hurry?'

Soon it was running parallel with some train tracks. A train came along blowing its whistle so the river tried to race it. Suddenly the smell of salt came into the air and the river saw what it had been hurrying for. The sea ! ! Soon fresh water mixed with salt water. It was the estuary. The river had met the sea it jumped about playing happily with the sea causing little waves. It ran up onto the beach running fast forwards then backwards then it found that the tide was going out so it went with it.

I can no longer carry on with this story. For this story was about a river but now it is part of the sea.

CATHERINE LILL (AGE 8) CHILDREN AS WRITERS 1980 (HEINEMANN)

Discuss pollution of water with the children. What do they understand by this term?

(Middle Infants at the Down County Infant School in Bexhill were on the right lines when they told me that pollution was 'bad sort of water', and that the water 'might be poisonous'. One lad knew right away that chemicals were responsible although he thought that doctors put chemicals in the water. Other children felt that jellyfish were the culprits.)

Have the children noticed any rubbish-strewn lakes or ponds in their neighbourhood? Visit a lake or pond and prepare a similar report to the river report outlined above. An abundance of plant and insect life in a stretch of water is an indication that the water is clean. If there is evidence of pollution then it should be reported to the National River Authority or the local Environmental Health Officer. (In 1988 there were 23,000 reported pollution incidents in Britain.) A class letter could be composed with everyone deciding how it should be phrased. Alternatively, if all is clean and healthy, a letter to the local paper reporting the findings would be a useful exercise.

How do we ensure that all the water that reaches us is clean and healthy? Talk the children through the different stages represented by the diagram below. Make sure that they understand what is happening at each stage of the process. Better still, if it is possible, arrange to visit a waterworks and see the system in operation.

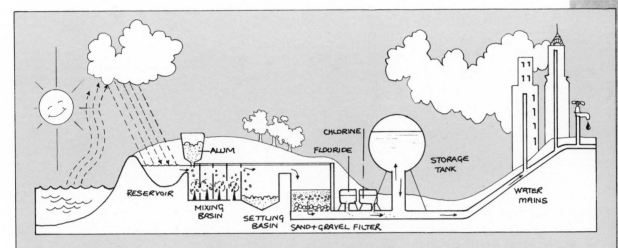

Water Cycle Chart

1. Water evaporates from lakes, rivers and oceans.
2. Clouds of water vapour form in the sky.
3. Rain falls to earth. Some falls into streams.
4. Some streams run into city's reservoir.
5. In mixing basin dirt and mud sticks to alum clumps.
6. In settling basin, clumps of alum and dirt sink to the bottom.
7. Sand and gravel filter takes out last impurities.
8. In pipe to storage tank fluoride is added for strong teeth. Chlorine is added to kill every last disease germ.
9. Pure water is held in a storage tank.
10. Water mains carry the water under the streets . . .
11. . . . to our homes and buildings.

Once you have talked the children through this process, prepare a set of cards with each stage of the treatment process being written down or illustrated on a separate card. Shuffle the cards and let groups of children attempt to sequence them again. This should result in some useful talk as different members of the group try to justify their reasoning.

Try to obtain a copy of *The Magic Bus at the Waterworks* by Joanna Cole (Kingfisher Books). This tells the story of a class trip with a difference when Ms Frizzle, the strangest teacher in the school, takes her class on a magic excursion through the waterworks. Along the way, the children learn what happens to the water as they swim through the purification system. The story is accompanied by pages from a science notebook giving us useful water facts about the different stages.

In the last line of his poem 'Water', Charles Thomson asks *'Where would we all be without it?'* Talk to the children about this. What would happen if we forgot to make water available for the class gerbils or water the plants? Remind the children that all living things need water. Farmers need water for animals to drink, human beings need to drink six large glasses of water each day (although much of this will be acquired through drinking tea, fruit juice, soup etc.) and crops need water to flourish.

The Summer of 1990 was a particularly dry summer. Check that children are familiar with the concept of drought. What happens in a drought? Can children remember any measures that were taken to combat the real threat of a drought in Britain?

Read Ann Bonner's description of what it was like:

Summer 1990 (Drought)

Do you remember rain?
Do you remember summer rain falling steadily from grey clouds, covering everything with a soft film of raindrops?
Do you remember wet grass and dripping leaves and roses, heavy, bent with rain?
Do you remember the smell of those first raindrops hitting the dry, dusty, parched ground? How everything turns green again with the rain and begins to grow afresh? How new it feels, after the rain?
Can you imagine no more rain?
The leaves are falling already. They lie crisp and brown on paths and pavements. Apples wither on the trees, tired of trying to grow fat and rosy.
Flowers droop. The straw-coloured grass is burned and brittle. The glorious sun shines, and shines. The sky stays blue, always blue, except for sometimes a few wispy, white clouds.
A perfect summer.
Yes — but for the want of the rain. The beautiful, cool, thirst-quenching rain.

ANN BONNER

Read the piece again and ask the children to listen out for drought words — dry, dusty, parched, wither, droop, burned, brittle. What do they all mean? Pick out words and phrases that tell us about the rain — *'falling steadily', 'soft film of raindrops',* the *'beautiful, cool, thirst-quenching rain'* etc. Suggest that children think of before and after pictures to illustrate Ann Bonner 's writing. Contrast 'before the rain' with 'after the rain': the dry, dusty landscape with the time when everything turns green again. Some children might prefer to write word pictures, others may like to annotate their pictures with appropriate words from the above description or with new words that they think of themselves.

Rain for Christmas by Richard Tulloch, illustrated by Wayne Harris, (C.U.P. 1989) describes a Christmas in Australia that comes in the middle of a drought. There is very little water available for Sally's family and even less to spare for the kangaroo, emu and cockatoo which visit Sally. So Sally writes a very important letter to Father Christmas. She tells him that she doesn't want any presents on Christmas Day and that all she would like him to do is to make it rain. Santa responds to her request by bringing a giant snowball to Australia!

This is a lovely story to read aloud and it emphasises the notion that drought is a world-wide problem, one which is often far more serious in overseas countries resulting in severe water restrictions, crop failure and even loss of life.

Discuss how in some countries water has to be collected from wells that are often some distance away. Ask children to imagine themselves fetching all the water their family needs each morning before school, just as many children have to do in countries such as Nigeria:

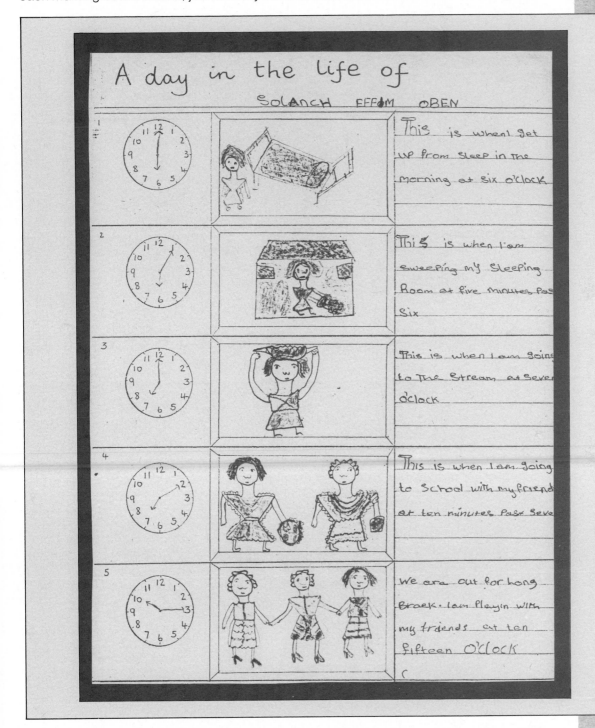

An average British family uses 568 litres of water a day. Measure out one litre and then imagine having to fetch 568 times as much using buckets and bowls. It is, of course, an impossible task and families in these countries have to make do with much less.

Sometimes too, the water isn't as clean as it should be. Statistics say that up to 22 million children die each year from waterborne diseases or lack of water. Thus education is important and all children must learn about hygiene in school.

Kamala Singh is eight years old and lives in Patagaon, a small mountain village in Nepal. The village has no running water and Kamala must help her mother fetch water from the river several times a day. She gets up before sunrise and is at school between 6 o'clock and 8 o'clock where as well as reading, writing and counting, she learns plenty of useful things for daily life. She learns how important it is to keep the house and yard clean. She also learns why she must always remember to wash her hands before eating and to boil water before drinking it or using it to prepare food. If she forgets to do any of these things she could make herself ill, along with other members of her family.

Tell the children about Kamala and how important good hygiene is when it is a matter of life and death. Good hygiene is also important in our homes and schools for we can still be made ill if we are careless. In groups the children could talk about or list rules for hygiene at home and in school. Work towards the production of an agreed class list which can be written up as a poster and displayed to remind children of good practice.

What can the children discover about improvements being undertaken in many countries so that the effects of unsafe water and bad sanitation can be minimised? Charities such as Oxfam, Unicef and Save the Children concern themselves with providing a clean, fresh piped water supply to villages in countries where it is needed. Most charities are happy to supply details of their work. Some children might care to write letters themselves or a class letter could be composed seeking information. Perhaps the children can think of a way to raise money for charity so that more children in other countries can enjoy fresh water.

¥Save the Children
Mary Datchelor House, 17 Grove Lane, London SE5 8RD.

Seferina's thirsty. She shouldn't drink the water she carries so carefully on her head, because it's dirty.
But she will.
And seven miles over arid, broken ground to the nearest water is a long walk when you're only eight years old.
Even without ten litres of water.
Still, Seferina's mother needs her help. Because a family of seven needs more than three times that amount every day just to stay alive. And her mother can't carry it all on her own.
Both Seferina and her mother hope she'll one day go to school. But she can't, because her younger sisters aren't yet strong enough to fetch the life-sustaining water every day.
Today may be different.
Today she could get help from someone she's neither met nor heard of before. Someone who lives far away, where water is clean and plentiful.
Someone who can help give Seferina and her family water for life.
But this child doesn't know - as she struggles home, parched and weary under the weight of her burden - this day might bring a continuing source of life to her and her family.
Nor does she know that someone could be you.

The few hours Kamala spends at school are the most precious part of her day

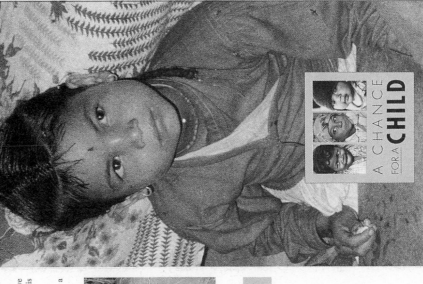

A CHANCE FOR A CHILD

In Nepal, 3 million children live in absolute poverty

Each year poverty means suffering for thousands of these children.

Of every one thousand babies born, 130 die before the age of one, and 202 die before the age of five. Because of diarrhoea, 45,000 children die each year. 50% of boys and 30% of girls are enrolled in primary school. But 73% of these schoolchildren do not finish their education. And 70% of those who leave school do so during the first year.

You too are aware of the injustice when a child cannot go to school, have access to medical help or grow up to be healthy because he or she is malnourished.

To help support children like these, please take part in the "A Chance for a Child" campaign today.

YES, you can do something for her, for him!

With your contribution, other Cheli Beti classes will be started, educational material will be provided, immunization campaigns will take place.

YOU CAN SAVE A CHILD FROM SUFFERING. HIS FATE IS IN OUR HANDS, IN YOUR HANDS

UNICEF UK

United Kingdom Committee for UNICEF
55, Lincolns Inn Fields - London WC2A 3NB
Telephone: 071- 405 55 92

Sources: UNICEF 1989. Photographies: UNICEF + B.Joliat. © APUI 1990.

Your gift can give many more children like Kamala a chance

Simply by supporting UNICEF today, you can bring a smile to the face of a child who longs for the chance to learn.

That is because your gift will help a child to write, read and do simple calculations.

More than this, it will help that child gain the knowledge he or she needs for a healthy life too - like why it is important to drink clean water and wash hands before eating.

With this vital - yet basic - knowledge, children in the developing world can grow up more confident of their abilities and start to change their own lives for the better.

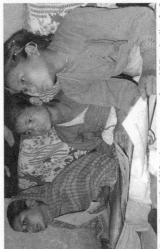

By sending a gift of £15 today, you can pay for a child's schooling for 2 months.

Better still, by making a regular gift of £7.50 a month, you can keep a child at school right through to the end of his or her education. And you'll be giving that child a gift of knowledge that will last for life.

To pledge a regular gift now, simply complete the Deed of Covenant and Direct Debit that you will find on the back of the enclosed donation form. Thank you.

UNICEF

"I am only 8 years old. What will my future life be?"

Kamala Singh lives in Patagon, a small village located high in the mountains in western Nepal. In this village, there are no roads, no running water, no electricity. There is certainly no medical help either.

Kamala, will she ever have her chance?

Up before sunrise

Kamala wakes up very early and gets up, full of energy, ready to start the day: she quickly slips into her skirt, blouse and "khasto", the shawl she wraps around her waist and which she sometimes uses to carry things. She carefully washes her hands and face then combs her hair. It is still dark outside. Where is she going so early?

School: a hope for the future.

A class for girls in the village was started four months ago. For the last four months, Kamala has discovered that life is more than just hard work from morning till evening. Life also means learning.

From 6 o'clock to 8 o'clock in the morning, she learns to read, write and count. She also learns plenty of other useful things for daily life: the importance of keeping the house and yard clean, the reasons for washing one's hands before eating, for boiling water before drinking it or using it for food preparation. These two hours at school are for her the best time of the whole day. But they fly by so quickly.

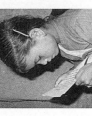

At school Kamala builds a foundation for her future.

SCHOOL: A CHANCE FOR NEPALESE GIRLS

"My days are so long"

Kamala returns home after school. Like the other little girls in her village, Kamala has to help her mother to fetch water from the river and wood from the forest, to take care of the cattle, to help in the fields and in the garden and to take care of her younger brothers and sisters.

Kamala goes to fetch water several times a day.

In the evening, Kamala is weary, but there is still the evening meal to prepare. And then when everyone has eaten, she washes the dishes with water mixed with ashes, out on the porch. Soap? That would be too expensive. Ashes cost nothing and are just as effective.

Long and exhausting, that describes Kamala's day. Even at the age of eight, it is common for girls to work up to seven hours a day. Most of them do not go to school. All this is because of a tradition that says that girls are more useful at home.

"Yes, I am tired," says Kamala, "but I really do love learning to read and write. When I am at school, I know why I'm there. What could I ever learn from buffaloes?"

By learning to read, write and do arithmetic at school, these girls are also learning to become aware of what they are capable of achieving. These are the Cheli Beti classes.

WILL KAMALA BE ABLE TO GO TO SCHOOL NEXT YEAR?

Cheli Beti means hope for a better life

In the region of Seti, at the extreme west of Nepal, UNICEF is promoting education through a special project: the Cheli Beti classes. These classes are given for 2 hours each day by one of the village women who has received special training.

Classes begin in November or December and continue for 160 days. Reading, writing, arithmetic and practical activities: the programme is full. For the first 75 lessons, learning starts with a series of simple words, each linked to a practical activity, for example: GHAR = house, KAHNA = food, PANI = water.

Then short sentences dealing with practical daily activities are introduced and illustrated. MHUKA DHUNE GARAUN = Wash your face. HATGODA SAPHA RAKHAUN = Wash your hands and feet.

The last ten lessons are devoted to more general subjects, directly related to the improvement of daily life: SANO PARIWAR, SUKHI PARIWAR = A small family is a happy family. PADEKI CHELI = An educated girl.

YOU CAN GIVE THIS HOPE TO A CHILD BY PARTICIPATING IN UNICEF'S WORK

Reading Resources

Poetry

A Very First Poetry Book (O.U.P. 1984) contains 'The River' by Clive Riche. *A Second Poetry Book* (O.U.P. 1980) contains 'Legging the Tunnel' by Gregory Harrison and 'The Plug-hole Man' by Carey Blyton. *Another First Poetry Book* (O.U.P. 1987) contains 'The Muddy Puddle' by Dennis Lee and 'I am the Rain' by Grace Nichols. All these are compiled by John Foster.

You'll Love This Stuff — Poems from many cultures selected by Morag Styles (C.U.P. 1986). This contains a section 'Water Water Everywhere' which includes poems about rain, storms, the monsoon etc.

Fiction

Grasshopper and the Poisoned River by Jim Slater (Granada 1982). Graham Hooper, nicknamed Grasshopper, swallows magic sweets, shrinks to 6cm high and is the champion of all creatures in danger. In this story he solves the mystery of the poisoned river with help from Jasper the rat and Jacob the tawney owl. Recommended for 7-8 year olds.

Ponders by Russell Hoban (Walker Books, 1988). Short stories depicting incidents in the lives of eight creatures who live around a country pond.

The House that Sailed Away by Pat Hutchins (Bodley Head and Fontana Lions). It rains every day when Grandma comes to stay until finally the house is wrenched from its foundations and floats away.

Webster's Walk by Jill Dow (Frances Lincoln 1990): in the Windy Edge Farm series. The ducks' pond has dried up so Webster decides to lead them to the river where a storm blows up.

Non-fiction

Books for Keeps: September 1988 — an extensive list of books on the theme of water.

Junior Education: April 1987 — Rivers, July 1983 – Water.

Junior Projects: No. 45 — Water.

Naturewalks: By the Canal by Jakki Wood (Hodder & Stoughton 1989). Part fiction, part fact. The story of a walk along the canal combined with information about discoveries.

Nature Watch: The Living Pond by Nigel Hester (Franklin Watts 1990). First-rate information book covering types of ponds, creatures that live in or near ponds and how to protect ponds.

Starting Points: Water by Su Swallow (Franklin Watts 1990). Excellent photography and clearly laid out text covering many aspects of water. A worthwhile first information book for young children.

Stream: Through the Seasons by Deni Brown (Wayland 1989). The changing stream over the course of a year plus ideas for activities.

Water by Brenda Walpole (A. & C. Black 1988). This book covers the many uses of water. It also explains in simple terms how fresh clean water reaches our homes and what happens to the water once it has been used.

Water Watch: Discover creatures that live in, on or near water by Dick King-Smith (Puffin 1988). Popular children's author gives advice on where to watch for animals, insects and birds at various watery habitats.

Waste and Recycling

A Naturalist found 77 mammals trapped in bottles around one lay-by on the A5.

If we stacked them end to end, all the aluminium cans that we use each year in Great Britain would stretch to the Moon and back.

How do the children feel about waste? What items are wasted? Do they own up to wasting anything themselves — food, water, paper etc. Ask children to make lists of ten things that their own families throw away each week. Similarly check the classroom litter bin and those on the school playground. (Warn that gloves should always be worn when handling litter and hands washed afterwards.)

Make a display of items that are regularly thrown away — a pile of cans, various bottles, all sorts of crisp packets, sweet wrappers, food cartons, yogurt pots, polystyrene trays, newspapers, magazines, etc. Again emphasise cleanliness.

Read some of Elizabeth Beresford's *Womble* stories. Most children will be familiar with these creatures and their philosophy. Final chapters of *The Wombles at Work* find the furry creatures living in Hyde Park faced with the Great Pollution Problem caused by a mountain of rubbish that is left over from a pop concert. Various ideas about recycling are introduced too.

Carry out a 'Womble Hunt' in the school grounds. Where can children find the most litter? Are there enough bins and are they in the right places? Are they the right design or is it easy for the rubbish to spill out or be blown away on windy days? Do children make use of what bins are available or do they forget when they're caught up in the hurly-burly of playtime? Can children design bins that might be more effective? Talk about the designs and assess good and bad points.

Does any rubbish find its way into the school grounds? If so, consider where it comes from. Perhaps there are nearby shops where sweets and canned drinks are purchased. Does this litter travel into the school grounds? Watch what happens when the refuse men call, particularly if it's a windy day. Does any rubbish escape and if so, is it always picked up again? Do you ever find that any larger items of rubbish have been dumped?

Extend your survey to neighbouring streets. Predict the sort of rubbish you will find and where you will find it. Mark on a map any places where there is a lot of rubbish — an area of wasteground, a building site, the garden of an empty house, close to local shops etc. Is there an area of wasteland which could be tidied up?

Suggest that the children write letters to the local paper or to a council official, either as a class or individually, giving details of their findings and putting forward proposals.

> Five Ashes C.E. School
> Five Ashes
> Mayfield
> E. Sussex
>
> 7th June 1990
>
> Dear Sir,
>   Yesterday my class split in half and half went down the road and half went up the road litter collecting. The group that went up the road I was in. We saw that there were no bins between the school and the entrance to Queens Mount so please could we have one or two bins along there please. And by the swings could we have another bin or a bigger one please. The one by the car entrance moved to the people entrance.
>   yours sincerely
>   Lucy Palmer
>   (aged 8)
>
> ✓
> lovely.

LUCY PALMER, FIVE ASHES SCHOOL

Who suffers in a rubbish-strewn environment? Tell the children about a naturalist's findings in the A5 lay-by (see above quote). This is almost certainly happening wherever we find rubbish. Mice, voles and shrews can all become trapped in glass jars and bottles, having been encouraged to investigate by the smell of food or drink. Broken glass or the sharp edges of cans can injure larger animals.

Five and six year olds in Christchurch C.E. School, St. Leonards were aware of the hazards posed to wild creatures. They very quickly produced a range of ideas that they felt might deter the would-be litter lout: 'Ring the police', 'Tell them that it's cruel', 'Make a sign — *Don't chuck rubbish on the ground'*, 'Make a sign with a picture of an animal caught in something'. Would any of these suggestions prove effective? What else could be done?

Improvisational drama might involve a situation where someone is seen dumping litter. Perhaps an elderly lady has seen what has happened from her window and decided to ring the police. Decide where this is happening. What would the lady tell the policeman and what would be his reply? Act out the situation. Think of other situations — teenagers smashing bottles, a man dumping a mattress from the back of his car. Again, think of what might be said.

Apart from safety considerations, it is also very unpleasant to travel to a local beauty spot and find ourselves surrounded by other people's litter. Have the children visited anywhere like this when they have been out for a day or on holiday? The *Tidy Britain Group* produce a poster of a British Beach with the slogan: *Please leave nothing but footprints* (see resources section). Can the children think of designs and slogans for posters that might encourage others to be more thoughtful in parks, by lakes, in lay-bys, etc?

The Rubbish Monster

Rodney Smithers, litterbug,
inside his bunkbed, warm and snug,
dropped some wrappers on the floor
and settling down, began to snore.
In dreams, he wandered round a fair
strewing litter here and there.
He guzzled candy floss and pop,
ate crisps and sweets, a lollipop,
and dropped each wrapper on the ground.
All at once he turned around
to see the rubbish that he'd thrown
had come to life; a giant had grown.
It loomed enormous to the skies
with cardboard feet and tins for eyes
and mouth just like a football goal.
It bent and swallowed Rodney whole.
Rodney, shrieking, left his bed
and pinched himself. He wasn't dead.
He peered around his bedroom floor.
Yes, litter lay there as before
and, yes, there was a litter bin.
He grabbed his rubbish — stuffed it in.
Next day he roamed about the town
observing rubbish with a frown.
He stood outside the supermart
and lectured sternly, hand on heart.

"Don't let litter swamp our land.
Pick it up please. Lend a hand.
Don't let the rubbish monster win.
Be tidy. Use a litter bin."

MARIAN SWINGER

Read the above poem through twice and then question the children to see whether they understand what has happened to Rodney. *The Rubbish Monster* is a poem that tells a story, and in this instance one with a moral. Can the children pick out the main points in the poem and sequence them? This could be done as a class or group activity, and when the order of events has been agreed upon, the poem could be represented in comic strip form: Rodney in his room surrounded by rubbish/Rodney wandering round the fair eating and dropping litter/The Rubbish Monster behind Rodney/A huge mouth about to swallow him/Rodney lying on his bedroom floor with litter everywhere/Rodney stuffing litter in the bin/Outside the supermart. Make sure that children pay attention to small details e.g. the *'cardboard feet and tins for eyes'* of the monster. Suggest that the children caption each section, either with a line from the poem or with words of their own. Perhaps they can add speech bubbles.

The above poem would also lend itself to interpretation through dance and drama. As Rodney wanders through the fair dropping litter, the items dropped might be brought to life by different children (appropriately garbed) who could then dance along behind him before merging into the Rubbish Monster. This 'fearsome' creature could then creep up behind Rodney before enveloping him. Further development could involve the children outside the supermart lecturing anyone passing by.

Some children might like to build their own rubbish monsters from some of the rubbish that they collect — the dustbin monster, the playground monster, the drink can monster etc. Can they think up stories to explain why their monsters come to life?

WOODLANDS CP SCHOOL, TONBRIDGE

Other children may enjoy designing litter disposal machines, perhaps for general refuse or for some specific problem — something with a long arm and magnetic hand that could clear away metal. Suggest that the children annotate their designs to explain what is happening.

If possible, ask along to the classroom people who deal with rubbish everyday. The school caretaker might have a number of suggestions as to how his job might be made easier, similarly with school cleaners. Perhaps a refuse man or a road sweeper might be persuaded to call in. Prepare questions in advance so that the most can be made from such visits.

A visit to the local public tip could give children an interesting insight into the sort of rubbish that is dumped everyday. Observe the tip for half an hour and notice how much rubbish is brought along for dumping. Observe who brings the rubbish. Note down the items of interest or make drawings. Is everything dumped in the same place or are there different areas for metal, for electrical goods, for garden refuse, for car tyres and so on? If this is the case, try to draw a plan of the tipping area showing where the various collection points are sited. Similar visits could be made to a scrapyard or to the corporation landfill.

At many public tips there are often people who sort through the rubbish as it arrives and select items that can be taken away and sold for recycling. As part of a project on waste, set up a recycling point in the classroom. Discuss what the process involves and how everyone can help. Perhaps the whole school will wish to help and a central collection point can be allocated. How aware are the children as to the kind of material that can be recycled?

Display items that can be recycled include aluminium cans (non-magnetic), bottles, paper, some plastics (often that used in drink bottles), scrap metal, old clothes (woollen fibres can be re-spun and made into new yarn). Produce posters for display around school to encourage others to collect items for recycling. Find out if there are bottle banks and collection points for cans near to your school. If these aren't obvious then older children might care to write to the council and enquire what facilities exist for recycling. Tell them about the school project.

Read *Sarah Scrap and Her Wonderful Heap* by Wendy Lewis (Cloverleaf/Evans Brothers 1990). Sarah Scrap inhabits a patch of wasteland in the middle of a town and is considered eccentric by the group of children who meet her. She collects the kind of rubbish that can be recycled, and the children help her to transport it to bottle banks, paper mills etc. Then once the site has been tidied, Sarah Scrap shows the children how to transform the waste area into a wild garden. 'Don't Sarah Scrap it, Sarah SAVE it!' she tells the children. The book will promote much discussion and should stimulate children into consideration of ways in which they can tackle recycling.

Ask children what happens to all the food waste in their homes. Does it go straight in the bin? Discuss how vegetable waste can be put on a compost heap to make fertiliser for the garden. If you have a school garden you could try setting up a compost heap so that the decomposed matter can be buried prior to growing plants. There are many good books available which offer guidance on the correct way to make compost.

Check that children know the type of recycled products that are available in the shops. A class of seven year olds who I talked with at St. Leonards C.E. School thought that you could buy recycled products in health food shops although only four children had ever visited one. No one knew that recycled products were available in many supermarkets but with some prompting guessed that the items available would be tissues, toilet rolls, kitchen towels etc. One lad was also aware that recycled writing and drawing paper could be purchased at a stationers.

Old clothes undergo a form of recycling when they are sent to jumble sales or given to charity shops. Money can be raised for charity or the clothes can be sent to countries where people need them. If it is possible, a small group might care to visit a charity shop to list the kind of goods that can be sold to raise money. Perhaps one of the volunteer helpers might be interviewed as to what happens in the shop and where the money goes. Many charity shops will also accept collections of used postage stamps, silver foil or even ring pulls from cans as these items help to make money too. Again, set up collection points for these around the school and make sure people know where they are.

One way of increasing school awareness of what can be done is to hold an assembly where as much information as possible can be given out to the other children so that they are encouraged to join in with the recycling programme. Decide what must be said and how to say it. Produce banners, posters and leaflets. Then, at some later stage, lead children to question the effectiveness of their efforts. Are other children more aware now than prior to the assembly? Did they get a good response and was this reflected in the amount of material that was brought to school?

Perhaps this song by Judith Nicholls might help to achieve a good response:

Recycling Song
(You all know the tune . . .!)

What shall we do with our old glass bottles,
What shall we do with our old glass bottles,
What shall we do with our old glass bottles,
Early in the morning?

Bring them to the bottle bank, RECYCLE,
Bring them to the bottle bank, RECYCLE,
Bring them to the bottle bank, RECYCLE,
Early in the morning!

Where shall we take our carrot peelings,
Where shall we take our carrot peelings,
Where shall we take our carrot peelings,
Early in the morning?

Put them on the compost heap, RECYCLE,
Put them on the compost heap, RECYCLE,
Put them on the compost heap, RECYCLE,
Early in the morning!

What shall we do with our old newspapers,
What shall we do with our old newspapers,
What shall we do with our old newspapers,
Early in the morning?

Take them to the paper-bank, RECYCLE,
Take them to the paper-bank, RECYCLE,
Take them to the paper-bank, RECYCLE,
Early in the morning!

What shall we do with the litter-throwers,
What shall we do with the litter-throwers,
What shall we do with the litter-throwers,
Early in the morning?

Drop'em on the compost heap, RECYCLE,
Drop'em on the compost heap, RECYCLE,
Drop'em on the compost heap, RECYCLE,
Early in the morning!

JUDITH NICHOLLS

Reading Resources

Poetry

'The Dustbin Men' by Gregory Harrison, included in *A First Poetry Book* compiled by John Foster (OUP 1979).

Fiction

Goanna by Jenny Wagner (Viking Kestrel). An Australian Conservation Foundation Book concerning a large goanna (lizard) and his flight from the bulldozers that threaten his home.

Non-fiction

Earthwatch: Waste and Recycling by Barbara Taylor (A. & C. Black 1990). A well-written, well-illustrated reference book for lower juniors. Half of the book looks at the waste we make and the other half shows how we can think more about recycling.

A selection of free leaflets: *Litter — A problem we can solve,* available from The Tidy Britain Group, The Pier, Wigan WN3 4EX.

Junior Education: Waste (Topic Pack — July 1990).

Endangered Animals

IDEAS in this chapter are an extension of those already considered as part of 'The Countryside' and will focus on animals that are not indigenous to Great Britain. A visit to a zoo or safari park which strives towards creating environments similar to animals' natural habitats may prove useful.

Prior to any visit spend a lot of time talking about animals. If possible, bring small animals to school as the wide variety of shapes and sizes can lead to much discussion. Discuss, in advance, the right ways to travel with animals so that they are not subjected to any unnecessary stress. Consider the right ways to handle small creatures. Encourage children to offer ideas as to how one animal differs from another. Consider movement, senses, body covering (fur, feathers etc) and feeding. Cards could be produced with collections of words for movement — slow, stealthy, gliding, jerky, scuttling, quick etc or for different physical characteristics e.g. types of beaks — short and stubby, long and slim, hooked, jagged edge etc. These could then be matched with the various creatures in the classroom or with pictures of animals from magazines or books. Help children to annotate any drawings that are produced. Coloured posters can serve to familiarise children with larger animals as can a display of model animals. (*Is It a Tiger?* by Mark Burgess, Methuen 1987, is a mix and match book which introduces young children to a variety of animals.)

Some children may enjoy writing about an animal in the form of a riddle (see the poem 'Hidden Creatures' by Anita Marie Sackett in 'The Countryside' chapter). Write short lines and attempt rhyme if children wish, although this may prove difficult for many. An easier approach is to concentrate on the clues and speak with the creature's voice:

Where I live it is very cold, but I don't need central heating to keep me warm, I have lots of thick white fur. Who am I?

I soar up high in the sky. I spot my prey from far away until down I swoop to grasp it with my sharp talons. Who am I?

Produce animal alphabets from the simple A for Anteater, B for Bear etc to those that encourage alliteration (poetic licence permitted!) e.g. Anteater eating ants/bear biting bananas/chimp chewing chocolate/donkey dieting/elephant enjoying eggs/flamingo feasting/gorilla guzzling etc. (A lovely source of inspiration for this kind of activity is *A Comic and Curious Collection of Animals, Birds and other Creatures* by Bobbie Craig, Ladybird Books 1981.)

Some children might care to make collections of animal sayings which could then be illustrated and displayed — proud as a peacock, a bear with a sore head, a bull in a china shop, stubborn as a mule, snakes alive, cock and bull story, brave as a lion etc. Collective nouns could also be illustrated — a pride of lions, a plague of locusts, a pack of wolves etc.

Consider also, the needs of animals. What factors are necessary for animals to stay alive? Are these true of all animals? Compare two very different creatures e.g. a sloth and a cheetah, a rabbit and an eagle etc — what do they need to keep them alive?

Examine the concept of adaptation in the natural world. Think of animals that have adapted for survival in various extremes of climate. Look at Arctic creatures — seals are insulated from the icy temperatures by thick layers of blubber. Polar bears and a whole range of creatures from fish to insects have chemicals inside them that enable them to survive in the Arctic wastes. Polar bears also have thick fur to protect them from the icy blasts and will hibernate in snow caves. Make comparisons with creaures that live in hot areas of the world. Many creatures have adapted for life in deserts. Gerbils, fennec foxes and jerboas all rest in burrows during the day before emerging at dusk to look for food. Camels store fat in their humps to provide them with food and water when both are scarce.

Suggest that children work on word/phrase chains, firstly building up a picture of a creature's habitat, then trying to match it to any adaptations made by the creature. For example, habitat — hot, dry, dusty, yellow sand, blue sky, cacti. Adaptations — sleeping by day, living in burrows, hunting at night, development of sharp eyesight or large ears to assist with hunting.

Continue looking at how creatures adapt by considering those that change colour at a moment's notice. Chameleons are perhaps the best example although a number of flatfish such as plaice are able to change colour to blend in with the seabed.

Older children will be able to appreciate how everything in nature is interdependent. Animals have adapted to life in their own special places and if their habitat is destroyed then the balance of nature is upset and creatures that cannot adapt further are likely to perish. Some work on simple food chains might well be appropriate here, and again, word/phrase chains could be developed to describe how the animals might feel about their homes before and after disturbance. For example the word/phrase chain for a wader might be — long legs, wading, cool water, long thin beak, probing mud for food, good place to rest and raise young: and when the wetlands are drained for development — no mud, water gone, food gone, lots of houses all around, can't feel safe anymore.

An extension of the above might lead to children talking and perhaps writing about how they might feel if a wild or special place were to be destroyed or developed. Focus on somewhere that children know. How would they feel if their homes were destroyed? Some of the writings by people whose homes were destroyed in the London Blitz might be appropriate here although the material would need to be chosen with discretion.

What do young children understand by 'Extinction'? I asked five and six year olds at the Down County Infants School in Bexhill. One lad was on the right track: 'Extinct means they're going to die,' although his reasoning, 'they've got a bad sickness' was off target. (There was much publicity in the papers about mad cow disease at the time and this had influenced his thinking.) When I asked why creatures were likely to become extinct there was general agreement that people killed them. 'They kill them because they're mean and cruel.' I asked what hunters wanted from the animals they killed — 'Skin . . . skin to make clothes.'

Perhaps the best approach to the notion of extinction with young children is to talk about dinosaurs. Models and pictures can be brought to school and discussed. Most children will be aware that there are no dinosaurs alive today. Some interesting theories might develop from asking the children to write about what they think happened to the dinosaurs. Some stories may touch on scientists' explanations and these can then be examined. Do ensure, however, that children understand that the dinosaurs became extinct because of natural changes that took a long time to happen, whereas today animals are threatened by changes brought about by people in a relatively short space of time.

Look at other creatures that are no longer alive today. Talk about the dodo, the quagga, and the great auk (see fact boxes).

The Dodo: The dodo was a giant flightless bird about the size of two turkeys. Home for the dodos was a group of islands off the east coast of Madagasgar including the island of Mauritius. Portuguese sailors first visited Mauritius in 1507 and because the dodos had no fear of people, the sailors easily caught them and slaughtered them for food. Almost a century later Dutch sailors did the same. Rats and cats also came ashore from the ships and more and more were left behind. Dodos nests were on the ground and their eggs and chicks became easy prey to these predators. By 1680 there were no more dodos on Mauritius.

The Quagga: The quagga appeared to be a mixture of horse and zebra but was, in fact, a unique species in its own right. It was native to Southern Africa and about the size of a small pony. Vast herds of quaggas were slaughtered by invading settlers in the 1840s and 1850s. Quagga meat could be fed to servants and its hide made into storage sacks. By 1880 the quagga was extinct.

The Great Auk: This was a swimming bird, in fact, the original penguin with a white breast and a black back. Great Auks lived on small islands off the Newfoundland coast, in the Gulf of St. Lawrence, and the tip of Nova Scotia. They were hunted for their feathers when there was a shortage of duck feathers which had previously been used to fill pillows and feather beds. In less than a century they were wiped out.

Suggest that the children draw pictures of these creatures and write, in their own words, how they became extinct. They might also invent their own animals, drawing them first and then describing how they looked. Could they then make up a story to tell how the animal became extinct. This could be based on what children have already learnt. Perhaps specific features could be noted to show how the animal had adapted to where it lived. Is there a link here as to why it died out?

What do the children know about animals that are in danger of extinction today? How are they being threatened with extinction?

Examine the threat posed by over zealous hunting. Many children will probably be aware of the plight of elephants and how their tusks are sold so that ivory ornaments can be made from them.

Elephant's Tusk, written by John Hare and illustrated by Eva Gundersen (Hodder and Stoughton 1990) is one of four books that attempt to heighten awareness of the plight of endangered species by means of story-telling. It will raise many questions about the nature of hunting and why creatures such as the elephant are labelled 'endangered'. Some children might care to relate the story of Toron Giwa and his great ivory tusks in their own words or to make up another adventure in which he nearly falls prey to hunters. Alternatively the story could be acted out.

Many zoos and wildlife parks operate schemes where animals may be fostered by classes of children who collect money to help pay for the upkeep of their particular animal. Much work can then be focused on a study of the animal's characteristics and requirements. It is also possible to foster baby elephants in Africa through a scheme set up by *Care of the Wild.*

We have fostered an elephant,
Ndume is his name.
He lives in the African jungle
And now he's really tame.
He lives by the river,
He plays in the mud.
He sometimes squirts water all over his head
and his tail can give you a thud.
But once he was really sad
Because his herd were shot
By greedy men called poachers
Who left them there to rot.
But first they stole their tusks
To sell as ivory for money.

VERITY STONE AND ALEXANDRA SMITH (AGE 8)

In the same series as *Elephant's Tusk* is *Rhino's Horn.* This tells the story of a baby rhino who is captured by men who wish to use his horn to make 'magic medicine.' Below, Bernard Young writes about the Javan rhino which is the world's largest rare animal living on land. It has been hunted for its horn over many centuries and may well become extinct soon.

The Javan Rhino

The Javan Rhino
(Rhinoceros Sondaicus)
really does weigh a tonne.

He's surprisingly shy and gentle
and was not born
to face a gun.

He hides
in the Javan jungle
and prefers to be alone

So don't go hunting
for him —
leave him on his own.

Leave him free
to wallow
in water and in mud.

That's the way
he likes it.
Is that understood?

BERNARD YOUNG

Where is Java? Who can find it first in the atlas? How do the children feel about people who slaughter elephants and rhinos? What happens to the baby animals if their mothers are killed? Which other animals are hunted to provide luxuries for people to buy? Talk about tortoises and how millions are taken from Africa to Europe in terrible conditions, with those left alive after the journey being sold as pets.

National parks and reserves can help to save hunted animals such as the rhino from extinction, although when there are only a very few remaining, confinement in zoos may be the only answer. Ask the children about their views on zoos — their good and bad points. Some children may be able to relate anecdotes about things they liked at a zoo or conditions that worried them. Think about the changes that have taken place in the welfare of captive animals over the past century. Many animals are now kept in open enclosures where conditions are as close as possible to the sort of habitat that they would enjoy in the wild. Some zoos and safari parks rear animals that are in danger of dying out and then return them to the wild where they can breed again. Through seeing wild animals at close quarters we can learn more about them and begin to empathise with their fight for survival.

Children may like to design a rhino enclosure taking into account that rhinos need an indoor area as well as a large outdoor area in which to browse. They also excavate large hollows with their horns and hooves. These then fill with rain water or are filled by zoo staff so that the creatures can wallow. Check that children understand what is meant by the words 'browse' and 'wallow'. List other creatures that do likewise. Think about the sort of enclosures that would be required by other species. Design a gymnasium for chimpanzees or an aviary for parrots.

Many creatures face extinction through the loss of their natural habitat and their subsequent failure to adapt to changed circumstances. Consider the plight of the rainforests and how their destruction leads very speedily to the loss of natural habitat for thousands of species.

Facts about rainforests:

Over half of the world's rainforests have been cut down since 1945.

Although they cover only a small amount of the Earth's surface they are home to about half the world's species of plants and animals.

Life-saving drugs and new food products have been developed from rainforest plants.

Rainforests affect the world's weather. If too many trees are destroyed there could be adverse climatic change (a complicated area for young children although some may wish to find out specific details themselves).

Rainforests are being destroyed: a) to make room for more farming land, although the soil is not very good and soon more trees have to be felled for yet more land; b) so that land can be used for cattle and the beef sold cheaply to fast food chains; c) so that wood such as teak and mahogany can be used for furniture.

Very young children may be introduced to the subject of rainforests through work on the huge variety of creatures that live there. A visit to a zoo or safari park might focus attention on jaguars, leopards, snakes, treefrogs, parrots, gorillas, chimps, gibbons, sloths, tapirs and anteaters, among others. Ask children to think up questions that would lead to the kind of information that they wish to know about these creatures — where they live, what they eat, how they move, their appearance etc. Similar research can be carried out into the types of plants and trees that are indigenous to rainforests and these can be drawn as background to a frieze that portrays the teeming life of the regions. Always ensure that there is a world map or extra large atlas to hand so that areas of rainforest can be pointed out.

LITTLE RIDGE C.P. SCHOOL, ST. LEONARDS-ON-SEA

Older children can examine how particular creatures have adapted to life in the rainforest. The sloth lives high up in the trees and the green algae that grows on its fur helps with camouflage. Gibbons have long arms and fingers to help them swing from tree to tree.

Children may enjoy attempting to write as if they were a particular rainforest creature. The following examples may serve as stimulus material:

Toucan

(spoken in a rap rhythm)

I was chatting away quite happily
With my feathered friends in the family tree;
Flapping and rapping in the steaming heat
To the funky rhythms of the jungle beat.

When suddenly I heard the sound
Of timber crashing to the ground,
And all around was smoke and fire
Climbing upwards higher and higher.

So down I went to investigate
The reason for this dreadful state
And to my surprise what did I see
Was a gang of guys vandalising my tree.

I said, "What do you think you're doing
Causing all this rack and ruin?"
And they replied, "We're on a mission
These trees are due for demolition.

Now, bird-brain if you know what's best
You'll find yourself another nest,
But if you dare to stick around
You'll end up there down on the ground."

I cried, "Do any of you know
How long it took my tree to grow?
A bird-brained toucan I may be
But at least I know how to treat a tree!"

DEBBIE CAMPBELL

The Sloth

I really do not feel the need for speed.
A peaceful stillness is my only need.
Before I move I always dream and brood.
To move I must be feeling in the mood.

> They say I've algae growing on my hair.
> It may be so; I simply do not care.
> I rather like my colour tinged with green.
> It's surely safer to be green than seen.
>
> PETER ROSE AND ANNE CONLON

The above pieces could be read by groups or individuals using suitable voices. Few children these days will be unaware of rap rhythms, some will have tried to write their own. The *Toucan* rap can be practised and then set to a percussion beat using instruments such as tambours, sticks and shakers. By contrast, the Sloth requires slow careful enunciation. Can anything similar be written, perhaps as a class exercise — for example a rainforest rap with different creatures complaining about the way they are being treated. Don't worry if exact rhymes are difficult, near rhymes will often suffice.

Children at St. Peter's R.C. School in Sittingbourne wrote prayers for rainforest creatures when they began to understand that the existence of these creatures was threatened by continued felling of trees.

The Hummingbird's prayer

Dear God,
Please give me lots of beautiful flowers to feed from, for I am only a little hummingbird. Please protect all the animals that live in the canopy layer, and stop people cutting down our homes so our trees will last forever. Amen.

KATIE BROWN

The Monkey's Prayer

Dear Lord,
Help us monkeys if you please,
Don't let man cut down our trees.
Give us juicy bananas to eat,
Let us all enjoy the rainforests' treats.
Protect all my brothers and sisters.
Amen

CHRIS NUTLEY

Children might care to consider what it would be like to visit the rainforests. Plan a trip and decide on a destination. How will they travel? What will they take with them — clothes, medicine, equipment? Where will they stay? What will conditions be like? How will they travel around? What do they hope to see? Such considerations should promote much useful discussion. Then, either as a class or in groups, prepare a folder or book about the rainforest. Include maps, drawings, posters etc as well as written observations.

Creatures in other parts of the world are also under threat of extinction because of man-made changes to their natural habitats. Can the children think of examples? Golden eagles are rare in Britain due to the disappearance of many forests where the eagles would find food. The destruction of bamboo forests in China along with over-hunting in the past has led to giant pandas coming close to extinction. The increased need for farmland to meet growing food demands means that vast areas of glasslands are fenced off for cattle and crops are sprayed with pesticides and herbicides, driving away or killing unwanted 'pest' species. Often large areas of countryside are taken over for factories and consequently wildlife is forced to move away into areas where there is difficulty in finding suitable food. Drainage ditches and ponds, previously homes for frogs, are often filled in to make way for new farmland leaving frogs with nowhere to breed. Industrial pollution too, is a worldwide problem. Birds of prey at the apex of a food chain eat rodents or smaller birds, which in turn consume the insects that are poisoned by insecticide sprayed on crops. Thus the whole food chain is affected causing widespread damage.

Suggest that children work in groups in the library or with classroom resources to discover other creatures that are in danger of extinction. Are the reasons always the same? What can the children discover about whales and whaling? Why are whales hunted? Read 'The Song of the Whale' by Kit Wright (*Hot Dog and Other Poems*, Kestrel/Puffin). Listen to recordings of whale songs. A useful introduction to the plight of whales today is *My Friend Whale* by Simon James (Walker Books 1990). In this picture book, Simon has a blue whale for a friend. They go swimming together every night but then the whale disappears. Children can talk about what they think might have happened to Simon's friend. The book concludes with some useful facts about whales which could lead to further research.

Consider the use of huge nets by tuna fishing boats, resulting in the indiscriminate slaughter of dolphins and other creatures who become entangled in the nets. Many producers of tuna now ensure that the fish are caught with a pole and line where there is no danger to other forms of marine life. Can the children devise adverts or labels for food products such as tuna, which will let the customer know that the product has been produced without endangering the lives of other species?

Can the children find out about laws that have been passed in an effort to protect endangered animals? How do they feel about hunters who break the laws? A holiday makers' Guide to items that shouldn't be bought could be produced. This would advise against the purchase of goods made from animals that face extinction — bags, wallets, shoes etc that are made from the skins of reptiles, ivory souvenirs from elephant tusks, anything made from real animal fur, coral etc. Impress on the children that buying such products simply allows the trade to flourish. What sort of items might holiday makers be encouraged to buy instead?

Read the children John Burningham's *Oi! Get Off Our Train* (Cape 1989). A small boy dreams that his toy train is real and that it travels through the night picking up endangered creatures along the way. Each time the initial reaction from the travellers is 'Oi! Get off our train.' But once the creature explains his predicament he is allowed on board. The following suggestions may be useful when reading the book:

1. Prior to reading, show children the cover of the book and ask what they think the story is about.
2. Do they think they will like/dislike the story? Why?
3. Read the story and show pictures.
4. What *is* the story about?
5. What do children understand by the terms 'Endangered' and 'Extinct'?
6. Think of another creature that might ask to climb aboard the train — rhino, whale, crocodile, parrot, tortoise, panda, bison etc.
7. What reasons would these creatures give to explain why they want to join the train?
8. Talk about the ending. Was it satisfactory? Could children think of a different ending?
9. List questions that children might put to the author/illustrator, John Burningham. Find other books that he has written.
10. Make up a similar story with animals being taken on board a space rocket and transported to another world. What would be the problems with such a modern day Noah's Ark? Can children either dramatise their own stories or John Burningham's?

Suggest that children might care to make others aware of their findings concerning endangered animals, perhaps by means of an eye-catching display or a school assembly. Prepare a fact sheet that can be photocopied and then distributed. Decide what needs to be on the sheet and how it will be set out. Can the work be done on the word processor? Will there be an illustration to add impact? Make other children aware of the need for conservation through poems, stories, posters and perhaps some drama revolving around the rainforest visit (p 97). Let someone act as a traveller who has just returned from such a trip. Other children might act as interviewers and question the traveller about what she saw.

Children might like to become involved with conservation on a personal level. There are many groups working both locally and nationally. Many have youth groups for children to join. Some national addresses are to be found at the back of this book but for local organizations check for information at your nearest library. Hastings in East Sussex, for example, has a Natural History Society, an Urban Wildlife Group, an Environmental Forum, a Badger Protection Society and a Community Tree Care Project plus local branches of the Living Without Cruelty Campaign, Friends of the Earth, Greenpeace, National Trust, R.S.P.C.A., R.S.P.B., and W.W.F. Allow children to write letters asking what the organization offers for young people and how they might become involved.

Reading Resources

Poetry

(Not all the material in the following anthologies will be suitable for 5-8 year olds)

Headlines from the Jungle — Poems about Wild Animals edited by Virginia McKenna and Anne Harvey (Viking 1990). Not just another compendium of animal poems, rather one that focuses on the problems that are faced by animals in today's uncaring world.

Jungle Jingles and Other Animal Poems by Dick King-Smith (Doubleday 1990). Again the emphasis is on fun — 'The Jungle is a feasome place/to members of the human race.' Fans of Dick King-Smith's prose will enjoy his excursion into verse.

The Usborne Book of Animal Poems selected by Heather Amery (Usborne 1990). A fun collection including 'The Sloth' by Tony Charles.

The Way to the Zoo Poems about Animals chosen by David Jackson (OUP 1983). An excellent selection including sections on 'The Wilderness' and 'Extinction'.

Fiction

My Friend Whale by Simon James (Walker Books 1990). A small boy makes friends with a whale, swimming with him each night until one day the whale disappears. Sensitive introduction to the plight of whales.

Rainforest by Helen Cowcher (Deutsch 1988/Picture Corgi 1990). Rainforest animals sense approaching danger as their forest rings with the noise of powerful machines. Wonderfully illustrated, check out the howler monkey! Also by Helen Cowcher, *Antarctica* (Deutsch 1990) which looks at Emperor penguins, Weddell seals and Adelie penguins and wonders how much longer Antarctica will provide a safe habitat for these creatures. *Tigress* by Helen Cowcher (Deutsch) will be published in 1991.

The Last Dodo by Ann and Reg Cartwright (Hutchinson 1989). A delightful modern fairy tale about a greedy king who must have the last dodo's egg at any price.

The Wild Beast by Franz Berliner (Bodley Head 1990). How the crotchety wildebeest changed his name — and his nature — in the face of a great drought.

Tiger Trek by Ted Lewin (Bodley Head, 1990). A tiger on the hunt through the Indian jungle.

Tilly Mint and the Dodo by Berlie Doherty (Methuen 1988/Young Lions 1989). Tilly's dream of meeting a live dodo comes true with the help of her friend Mrs Hardcastle. A lovely story for 7 and 8 year olds. Contains 'The Song of the Last Dodo'.

When We Went to the Zoo by Jan Ormerod (Walker Books, 1990). Gibbons, orangutans, toucans, emus — a tour of the zoo. Just right for reception classes.

Non-fiction

Animals in Danger by David Taylor (Boxtree 1990). Here the reader becomes involved in obtaining the latest information on ten endangered animals prior to launching possible rescue missions. For good readers only.

Earthwatch: Trees for Tomorrow by Lynne Patchett (A. & C. Black, 1990). All sorts of trees plus a look at the disappearing rainforest. Good resource for 7-8 year olds.

Let's Go To A Safari Park by Janine Amos (Cherrytree Books 1989). Looking behind the scenes to discover how the animals are fed and cared for.

Life in the Rainforests by Lucy Baker (Franklin Watts 1990). Superbly illustrated and photographed. Serves as an excellent introduction to rainforests.

My Visit to the Zoo by Sophie Davies and Diana Bentley (Wayland 1989). Donna and her brother Jonathan visit Whipsnade Zoo where they meet, handle and help to feed a selection of animals.

Noah's Choice: True Stories of Extinction and Survival by David Day (Viking 1990). A marvellous read or simply for dipping into, too old for the age group here but teachers will find it a superb resource. Encouraging stories of creatures being brought back from the brink of extinction gives hope for the future.

Rain Forest Homes by Althea (CUP 1985). Informative and well-illustrated. A good non-fiction tie-in with Helen Cowcher's fictional *Rainforest* (above).

Save our Earth: Rainforest Destruction by Tony Hare (Franklin Watts 1990). Well explained and clearly illustrated. Again more suited to 7-8 year olds.

The Elephant Book by Ian Redmond (Walker Books 1990). Written for the Elefriends Campaign with a preface by Daphne Sheldrick. Again more a book for teachers although young children will appreciate the marvellous photography.

Usborne Conservation Guides: Protecting Endangered Species by Felicity Brooks (Usborne 1990). Useful guide to plants and animals facing extinction along with ways in which they can be helped. Some success stories too.

World Wildlife: Our World in Danger (Ladybird 1989). Produced in conjunction with WWF. A useful reference book with clear explanations of the many threats to wildlife.

Further Reading

Further Reading Resources for Teachers and Pupils

BBC Fact Finder: Earthwatch written by Penny Horton, Tony Potter and Dee Turner (BBC Books 1990). Well produced and well illustrated examination of environmental problems, from the ozone layer to rainforests, plus practical suggestions.

Dinosaurs and all that Rubbish by Michael Foreman (Hamish Hamilton 1972/Puffin 1974). Man leaves our polluted world to travel to the stars. Meanwhile dinosaurs re-colonise the Earth and tidy it up. Man is only allowed back when he agrees that the Earth should be shared and enjoyed by everyone. Again, this will probably promote a lot of questions.

Environmentally Yours: A Green Handbook for Young People produced by *Early Times* and Puffin (1991). Examines what is happening at the moment and what will happen if things carry on the way they are. Plus 'Towards a Better World' what we can do to help.

One World by Michael Foreman (Anderson Press 1990). A lovely book to share with children. The world of a rock pool is a microcosm of the world itself. Prepare for much discussion afterwards. (Also *Books for Keeps* No 62. May 1990 in which Michael Foreman writes about the 'slow emergence of *One World* in his article 'The Birth of a Book.')

The Blue Peter Green Book written by three members of the *Blue Peter* production team — Lewis Bronze, Nick Heathcote and Peter Brown (BBC Books/Sainsbury's 1990). An examination of the problems that beset the environment plus 'Action — How you can help' sections. Clear expalanation of the Greenhouse Effect.

The Children's Giant World Atlas compiled by Keith Lye (Hamlyn). A really useful resource when children want to know where the rainforests are or where the latest oil spill has occurred etc.

The Ozone Friendly Joke Book compiled by Kim Harris, Chris Langham, Robert Lee and Richard Turner (Beaver 1990). A wonderful antidote for anyone who finds themselves taking everything just that little bit too seriously. For example: *What do you call an inebriated Greek ecologist? Ouzo friendly!* Be warned!

The Young Green Consumer Guide by John Elkington and Julia Hailes, with Douglas Hill. Illustrated by Tony Ross and published by Gollancz 1990. A fascinating book that explores the issues and suggests ways in which individuals can help, both practically and through helping to raise awareness. Sections on home and school.

The Young Person's Guide to Saving the Planet by Debbie Silver and Bernadette Vallely (Virago 1990). Different forms of action that can be taken plus an A-Z of Green issues, from acid rain to zoos, from CFCs to VDUs. Good as a quick reference guide.

50 Simple Things Kids Can do to Save the Earth written by the Earthworks Group and published by Sphere Books (1990). Everything from being a bottle bandit to stamping out styrofoam, from being school-wise to joining the heat-busters, plus eco-experiments — make your own recycled paper etc.

Specifically for Teachers

Earthrights: Education as if the Planet Really Mattered by Sue Greig, Graham Pike and David Selby (WWF/Kogan Page 1987). Towards 'thinking globally' and 'acting locally'. Useful section 'Beginning Early' focuses on the need to lay the foundations for a *'planet-conscious education programme.'*

Greenprints for Changing Schools by Sue Greig, Graham Pike, David Selby (WWF/Kogan Page 1989). A review of how teachers and others involved in education have set about promoting global education in schools. *'Great oak trees can start in the nursery'.*

Learning Together: Global Education 4-7 by Susan Fountain (WWF/Stanley Thornes 1990). A practical handbook crammed with ideas for fostering self-esteem, promoting co-operation and developing communication skills, all concepts which help to prepare children for participation in strategies that help to develop global awareness.

My World (WWF in association with Scholastic 1990/91). A series of 16 page illustrated supplements exploring the local environment and making links with global issues. These are aimed at teachers of pupils aged 7-12 years and linked with National Curriculum programmes of study for Key Stage 2 in Science. The supplements are available as a free insert in the following issues of 'Junior Education' or alone from WWF. Exploring the Earth (Feb. '90), Exploring the Air (April '90), Exploring Water (July '90), Exploring the Weather (Oct. '90), Exploring Plants and Animals (Dec. '90), Exploring Ourselves (Feb. '91), Exploring Food (April '91), Exploring Energy (June '91), Exploring the Future (Oct. '91).

Poetry for Projects compiled by Pie Corbett and Brian Moses (Scholastic 1989). Practical ideas on a number of project areas including 'Conservation', 'Animals', 'Water', 'The Sea', 'Birds' and 'Ourselves'.

The Books For Keeps Green Guide to Children's Books. To be published Spring 1991, price £6.50 from *Books for Keeps,* 1 Effingham Road, Lee, London SE12 8NZ. A review of over 350 works of fiction and non-fiction with a 'green' theme plus articles on promoting environmental awareness in the classroom.

The Last Rabbit edited by Jennifer Curry (Methuen/Mammoth 1990) and *What on Earth . . .?* edited by Judith Nicholls (Faber 1989). Two anthologies of poetry on the theme of conservation. Much of the material will be unsuitable for the age group but both collections are worth searching through. The former contains 'Hurt No Living Thing' by Christina Rossetti and 'A Celtic Greeting' by Jane Whittle, while the latter features an anonymous piece 'Mummy, Oh Mummy' which would prove good assembly material.

The Primary School in a Changing World: A Handbook for Teachers edited by Jenny Burton (Centre for World Developmental Education 1989). Practical problems and advice re the development and implementation of a whole school policy on global education. Useful activity plans.

Useful Addresses for Resource Material

ALUMINIUM CAN RECYCLING ASSOCIATION, Suite 308 I-Mex House, 52 Blucher Street, Birmingham B1 1QU. Free information packs with teachers' files and leaflets.

CHRISTIAN AID, PO Box 100, London SE1 7RT produces *Focus on Water* — ideas for activities etc.

COUNCIL FOR ENVIRONMENTAL EDUCATION, School of Education, University of Reading, Reading RG1 5AQ.

FORESTRY COMMISSION, Public Information Division, 231, Corstorphine Road, Edinburgh EH12 7AT. *Environmental Threats to Forests* — available free.

FRIENDS OF THE EARTH, 26-28 Underwood Street, London N1 7JQ. A range of fact sheets for primary children including free leaflets on acid rain, agriculture, air pollution, energy, global warming, ozone depletion, recycling and water pollution. Also *The Friends of the Earth Yearbook* packed with facts, fun and games, positive things to do and experiments. Friends of the Earth are intending to start a teachers and schools membership scheme which will provide subscribers with educational material.

GREENPEACE, Greenpeace House, Canonbury Villas, London N1 2PN. Public Information Unit answers letters from all age groups, including young children (probably about 5% of all letters received are from under 10s). A fact sheet about Whales is available, along with a poster published by the Greenpeace Environmental Trust called *Where do we go to from here?* This introduces children to environmental terms and encourages them to identify the good things and the bad things that are going on in the world.

NATIONAL SOCIETY FOR CLEAN AIR, 136 North Street, Brighton BN1 1RG.

NATURE CONSERVANCY COUNCIL, Publicity Services Branch, Northminster House, Peterborough, PE1 1UA produces posters, wallcharts and booklets on all aspects of conservation.

NOISE ABATEMENT SOCIETY, PO Box 8, Bromley, Kent BR2 0OH.

ROYAL SOCIETY FOR THE PROTECTION OF BIRDS, The Lodge, Sandy, Bedfordshire SG19 2DL. Project guides, films and videos.

SAVE THE CHILDREN, Mary Datchelor House, 17 Grove Lane, Camberwell, London SE5 8RD. A pack entitled *Refugees* has been specifically created and tested with 7-8 year olds. It is designed to help children understand the concept of refugees and to encourage a positive attitude towards different communities and cultures. *Doorways* is a pack for 9-13 year olds which may be useful for introducing issues of homes and homelessness.

Also check out other material including *Resurrecting Rubbish, Trees for Life* and *Hope for the Earth* (about pollution).

THE CENTRE FOR ALTERNATIVE TECHNOLOGY, Machynlleth, Powys SY20 9AZ.

THE CONSERVATION TRUST, George Palmer Site, Northumberland Avenue, Reading, Berkshire RG2 7PW. Produces a set of 20 Junior Topic cards on various aspects of conservation.

THE TIDY BRITAIN GROUP, The Pier, Wigan WN3 4EX. A selection of free leaflets — *Litter, A Problem we can Solve.* Also *Our Environment,* a project for primary schools, plus a 40 frame filmstrip *Litter, Waste Management and Recycling.*

UNICEF UK, 55 Lincoln's Inn Fields, London WC2A 3NB. Educational materials tend to be directed at the 8-13 age range although UNICEF say that many teachers have adapted these for use with younger children. Of particular relevance are *Songs, Games and Stories from Around the World* (designed for children under 8) — book and cassette, although they may be purchased separately; *Clean Water: A Right for All* — active project work for 8-13 year olds — cross-curricular A4 project book; *We Are What We Eat, but who controls our choice?* — an active learning project on food and nutrition for 8-13 year olds, including photocopiable pupils' sheets and notes for teachers. Also available and co-produced with Save the Children are three project books for teaching about the Convention on the Rights of the Child for use with 8-13 year olds — *The Whole Child, It's Our Right* and *Keep Us Safe* plus Teachers' handbook.

WATER AID, 1 Queen Anne's Gate, London SW1H 9BT. Educational resource materials on water in the developing world.

WORLD WIDE FUND FOR NATURE (WWF) UK, Education Department, Panda House, Weyside Park, Godalming, Surrey GU7 1XR. Catalogue includes a large number of publications suitable for the 5-11 age range.

(When writing to any of the above addresses please enclose a SAE.)

Selected Educational Visits

NATIONAL TRUST PROPERTIES. Details about the educational services offered by the National Trust can be obtained by writing to The Education Office, The National Trust, 36 Queen Anne's Gate, London SW1H 9AS, or by telephoning the Education Manager on 071-222-9251. The Education Unit provides regional lists of properties that are most suited to educational visits. A Schools Corporate Membership scheme gives your class free access to every property. Also obtainable: *Cross-currents — A coastal studies handbook for teachers.* This is a collection of written and visual resources and much of the material will prove helpful in preparing and supporting coastal field trips.

For an introduction to conservation through first hand experience with animals, the following may well be worth visiting:

BELFAST ZOO, Antrim Road, Newtownabbey. BT36 7PN, Northern Ireland. Tel: (0232) 776277. Various packs available plus 'Zoo Crack' — a seasonal news sheet.

CHESTER ZOO, The North of England Zoological Society, Zoological Gardens, Chester CH2 1LD. Tel: (0244) 380280. Teachers planning a visit are encouraged to write or 'phone for the zoo's latest 'ZEST pack' which gives all basic details regarding a huge list of publications for all age ranges. Much material suited to 5-8 year olds. Particularly impressive is 'The Big Ones for Little Ones' — Elephants, Rhinoceros and Giraffe: A Teaching Pack recommended for the Infant Age Range.

DARTMOOR WILDLIFE PARK, Sparkwell, Plymouth, Devon PL7 5DG. Tel: (0755 37) 209. Includes the West Country Falconry Centre. Useful observation packs for 5-7 and 8-13 year olds.

DRUSILLAS ZOO PARK, Alfriston, East Sussex BN26 5QS. Tel: Information — (0323) 870656, Bookings (0323) 870234. Wide-ranging publications including 'Copycat' — an activity and art pack for 6 year olds and upwards and 'Zoo Pack' providing information on basic themes such as food chains, predators, prey, animals in danger etc. New attractions include Meercat Mound (designed by 11 year old children from Lewes), Monkey Mountain Sanctuary and the Rainforest Story.

DUDLEY ZOO, 2 The Broadway, Dudley, West Midlands DY1 4QB. Tel: (0384)252401. Two booklets 'The Zoo' and 'Our Day at the Zoo' are designed to meet the needs of 5-7 and 7-9 year olds respectively. Teachers' pack and guides also available.

JERSEY WILDLIFE PRESERVATION TRUST, Les Augres Manor, Jersey JE3 5BF, Channel Islands. Tel: (0534) 61949. Founded by Gerald Durrell in 1963 and deeply involved with carefully planned breeding programmes for selected species. A wide range of educational activities and support material is available plus 'The Dodo Dispatch', a newspaper for members of 'The Dodo Club' run by the Trust.

KILVERSTONE, The Latin American Zoo, Kilverstone, Thetford, Norfolk, LP24 2RL. Tel: (0842) 755369. Also includes Falabella Miniature Horse Stud. Houses many of Latin America's rarest mammals and exotic birds. Fact Packs and Teachers' Information Packs are available.

MARWELL ZOOLOGICAL PARK, Colden Common, Winchester, Hampshire SO21 1JH. Tel: (096274) 407. Impressive range of teacher resources including material on baby animals for 5-7 year olds, booklets for 7 year olds and above on such topics as 'Colour and Markings' and 'Rainforests', plus 'What Shall We Zoo?' — ideas for zoo-based activities. Of particular interest are 'The Marwell Drama Project' and 'The Marwell Cat Drawing Project' — both of these were written by teachers who were seconded to the Education Service at Marwell.

THE ZOOLOGICAL TRUST OF GUERNSEY, La Villiaze, St. Andrew, Guernsey, Channel Islands. Tel: (0481) 39176. Specialises in smaller mammals and birds with an emphasis on those from South America. A wide range of activity sheets and fact sheets are available for all ages.

TWYCROSS ZOO, East Midland Zoological Society Limited, Atherstone, Warwickshire. CV9 3PX. Tel: (0827) 880250 and 880440. Good range of resources and teaching sessions. 'Zoo-do' sheets offer ideas for interactive activities at the zoo and in the classroom. Of particular note — 'A Splash of Colour' a teacher's guide to animal colours and primary art.

WHIPSNADE WILD ANIMAL PARK, Dunstable, Bedfordshire LU6 2LF. Tel: (0582) 872171. 'Hands on' sessions with a variety of animals for 4-6 year olds. Tours and tape-slide presentations for older children plus 'Christmas at Whipsnade' — a special presentation during December!

Venues worth visiting in connection with other environmental activities:

CLEARWELL CAVES. Enquiries to R. Wright Esq., The Bungalow, Heywood Road, Cinderford, Gloucestershire, GL14 2QT. Tel: Dean 23700. The Forest of Dean's Mining Museum. Iron ore has been mined here for over 2,500 years. Guides angle information to suit schools' requirements.

COTSWOLD FARM PARK, Rare Breeds Survival Centre, Guiting Power, Cheltenham, Gloucestershire. GL54 5UG. Tel: (04515) 307. Also Bemborough Farm Trail. An Education Centre offers slides and quiz sheets.

EDINBURGH BUTTERFLY AND INSECT WORLD, Dobbies Gardening World, Lasswade, Midlothian. Tel: 031-663-4932. Insects include tarantulas and giant milipedes. Children are encouraged to handle many of the insects. Useful educational pack available.

GLODDFA GANOL SLATE MINE, Blaenau Ffestiniog, Gwynedd, LL41 3NB. Tel: (0766) 830 664. Educational pack consists of booklets explaining the history of slate mining and a detailed illustrated description of the workings in the mine caverns.

WIMPOLE HALL AND HOME FARM, Arrington, Royston, Herts. SG8 0BW. Tel: (0223) 207801. Rare livestock breeds, old farming methods and parkland natural history. Write or 'phone for Teachers' Survival Guide. Fact sheets, quizzes etc plus ten-minute educational video for 4-8 year olds.

WOOKEY HOLE CAVES, Wookey Hole, Wells, Somerset BA5 1BB. Tel: (0749) 72243. Also includes Papermaking, Madame Tussaud's Cabinet of Curiosities and the history of fairgrounds. Teachers' information pack available.

Acknowledgements

I should like to thank the following teachers who have invited me into their classrooms and/or offered help, advice and ideas, along with a number of schools that have allowed me to use work by children: Trish Vaughan and her children from Hollington Junior School, St. Leonards-on-Sea; Jane Saunders, Lesley Worsley and their classes, also Tom Collins, St. Leonards C.E. School; Maureen Harman, Little Ridge C.P. School, St. Leonards; Sue Densem and her children, Christchurch C.E. School, St. Leonards; Staff and children at Bexhill Down Infants, Bexhill-on-Sea; Gill Mills, Advisory Teacher for Special Education, East Sussex; Alan Shuttleworth, Hellingly Primary School and Lesley Pearson, Kingsmead C.P. School, Canterbury. Also St. Mary's R.C. School, Crowborough; Freda Gardham C.P. School, Rye; Middle Street C.P. School, Brighton; Coombe Road C.P. School, Brighton; Marshlands C.P. School, Hailsham; Woodlands Junior School, Tonbridge; St. Saviour's C.P. School, Westgate; St. Peter's R.C. School, Sittingbourne; Cuxton Infant School, nr.

Rochester; Wivelsfield C.P. School; Five Ashes C.E. School; Middletune Junior School, Sittingbourne; West Burton School, Leyburn, N. Yorkshire; West Cliff C.P. School, Whitby and to children from Gallery Young Writers, Rye. Thanks also to Jan Moore, Librarian, Herne Bay Library.

The following pieces of writing by children were award-winning entries in the W.H. Smith Young Writers' Competition and are reprinted by permission: 'The Little Trickle' by Catherine Lill (1980); 'The Song of the Sea' by Neil Richards (1981); 'Our Street' by Anatol Sleeman (1984); 'Me' by Flora Carnwath (1985) and 'The Blackberry' by Emily Byham (1988).

'Conkers' by Roland Nicholls was a prize winning poem in the 1986 Cadbury's Poetry Competition and is reprinted by permission.

'With my feet I can . . .' by Crystal Stainton appeared in the Kent anthology of children's writing *Steaming and Dreaming*.

Thanks are also due to the following: Frank Melling, Project Director of *In Our Own Words* and to Cheshire Education Authority for permission to print Peter's 'I love rain . . .' and James Hall's 'On the Farm'; Mr R. A. Dennett, Director of Tourism and Leisure, Hastings; Hastings and St. Leonard's Observer; UNICEF UK for information about Kamala Singh from their leaflet 'Chance for a Child'; Save the Children for information about Seferina.

Thanks and acknowledgement are due to the following writers for permission to publish original material: Ann Bonner, Tony Bradman, Stanley Cook, John Foster, David Harmer, Robin Mellor, Judith Nicholls, Anita Marie Sackett, Matt Simpson, Ian Souter, Marian Swinger, Charles Thomson, Bernard Young. Also to Wes Magee whose poem 'Christmas Day Walk' was previously published in *The Witch's Brew and Other Poems* (CUP 1989); to Stanley Cook whose poem 'In the Playground' was featured in *The Dragon on the Wall* (Blackie 1989) and to Gareth Owen for 'Leaving Home'.

All these pieces are reprinted by permission. Copyright of all prose and poetry remains with the authors.

A final thank you to Alison Manners (Education Officer) and Cherry Duggan (Publishing Officer) at WWF for their valuable advice.

If anyone feels that a credit has been overlooked I would be grateful if they would contact WWF so that the omission may be rectified in subsequent editions.

Brian Moses